NAGASHINO 1575

SLAUGHTER AT THE BARRICADES

SERIES EDITOR: LEE JOHNSON

CAMPAIGN 69

NAGASHINO 1575

SLAUGHTER AT THE BARRICADES

TEXT BY
STEPHEN TURNBULL

BATTLESCENE PLATES BY
HOWARD GERRARD

First published in Great Britain in 2000 by Osprey Publishing, Elms Court,
Chapel Way, Botley, Oxford OX2 9LP United Kingdom
Email: info@osprey-publishing.com

ISBN 1 85532 619 1

Editor: Marcus Cowper
Design: The Black Spot

Colour birds eye view illustrations by the Black Spot
Cartography by the Map Studio
Battlescene artwork by Howard Gerrard
Wargaming Nagashino by Arthur Harman
Origination by Grasmere Digital Imaging Ltd, Leeds
Printed in China through World Print Ltd

00 01 02 03 04   10 9 8 7 6 5 4 3 2 1

*For a Catalogue of all books published by Osprey Military, Automotive
and Aviation please write to:*
**The Marketing Manager, Osprey Publishing Ltd., P.O. Box 140,
Wellingborough, Northants NN8 4ZA United Kingdom
Email: info@OspreyDirect.co9.uk**

**The Marketing Manager, Osprey Direct USA, P.O. Box 130, Sterling
Heights, MI 48311-0130, United States of America
Email: info@OspreyDirectUSA.com**

Or visit the Osprey website at:
http://www.osprey-publishing.co.uk

Dedication

To Kazukata Ogino in recognition of his invaluable and
friendly assistance in the preparation of this book.

Artist's Note

Readers may care to note that the original paintings from
which the colour plates in this book were prepared are
available for private sale. All reproduction copyright what-
soever is retained by the publisher. All enquiries should be
addressed to:

Howard Gerrard, 11 Oaks Road, Tenterden, Kent,
TN30 6RD UK

The publishers regret that they can enter in to no
correspondence on this matter.

PAGE 2 **A warrior wearing a *horô*. The horô was a stiffened
cloak arranged round a bamboo framework, supposedly for
catching arrows, an entirely pointless exercise. In fact the
horô seems to have developed as an elaborate form of
sashimono favoured in particular by battlefield messengers.
Oda Nobunaga was served by two bodyguard regiments distinguished by red and black horô. It was from their ranks
that Nobunaga chose the commanders of the matchlock
units at Nagashino.**

PAGE 3 **A simple *jingasa* of lacquered leather, for a footsoldier. It was the mark of a successful general during the
Sengoku Period that he could handle the lower class troops
who were beginning to make up a large proportion of any
army. The introduction of simple armour for the footsoldiers
was an important development. The jingasa (literally 'war hat')
was usually conically shaped, and often of iron, although
some, like this one, were of strong lacquered leather.**

KEY TO MILITARY SYMBOLS

CONTENTS

大日本名将鑑

信玄の長子を勝頼と号す年十六歳にて
はや父信玄と諡られ其後父信虎
武略計を以て顕はす後父信虎
に諏訪村を破られ信玄呑吞良
忍び諏訪村にて走りと虎
虎と戦ひて年の久へ合川家に走られ
るとらとり武略諏訪図み当に
戦さとり武略諏訪図み当に
言ひ至り其と武さと向け野田の
薮入る虫の音にこゝへをに
ず敵の鉄丸にあふ天光年
四月卒す五三

6

ORIGINS OF THE CAMPAIGN

LEFT **This print by Yoshitoshi shows the moment when Takeda Shingen was mortally wounded by a bullet fired by a sentry during the siege of Noda castle in 1573. His death proved to be a tragedy for the Takeda family, when the leadership passed into the hands of his less talented son, Takeda Katsuyori. The depiction of the walls of Noda as a simple yamashiro style castle are not unlike the appearance Nagashino castle would have had in 1575. (Courtesy of Rolf Degener)**

Nagashino and the 'Warring States Period'

The siege of Nagashino castle and the battle of Nagashino which followed it make up one of the pivotal moments in the history of the samurai. Its military significance is considerable, because it demonstrated the power available through a skilful combination of arms, comparatively simple defensive measures and, above all, the use of firearms on a large and controlled scale. Other samurai leaders who later found themselves in a similar position would look for lessons that they could apply from the example of Nagashino.

The battle of Nagashino is but one among many conflicts of 16th century Japan. The period is known as the *Sengoku-jidai* (Warring States Period), a term borrowed from the Chinese dynastic histories. For the past five centuries Japan had been ruled by a succession of dynasties of Shoguns,

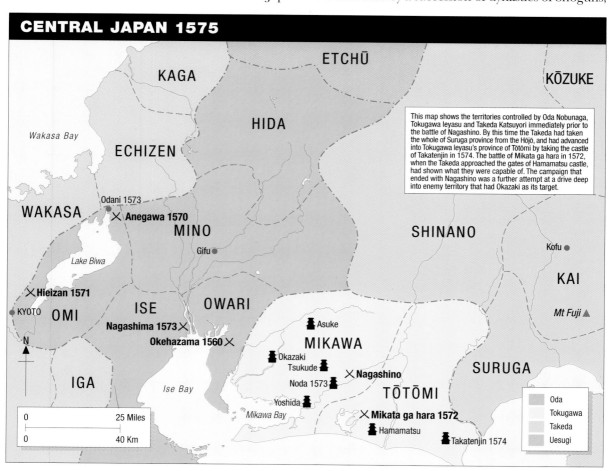

CENTRAL JAPAN 1575

This map shows the territories controlled by Oda Nobunaga, Tokugawa Ieyasu and Takeda Katsuyori immediately prior to the battle of Nagashino. By this time the Takeda had taken the whole of Suruga province from the Hōjō, and had advanced into Tokugawa Ieyasu's province of Tōtōmi by taking the castle of Takatenjin in 1574. The battle of Mikata ga hara in 1572, when the Takeda approached the gates of Hamamatsu castle, had shown what they were capable of. The campaign that ended with Nagashino was a further attempt at a drive deep into enemy territory that had Okazaki as its target.

ETCHŪ
KAGA
KŌZUKE
HIDA
Wakasa Bay
ECHIZEN
Odani 1573
✕ Anegawa 1570
MINO
SHINANO
WAKASA
Gifu
Kofu
Lake Biwa
KAI
✕ Hieizan 1571
OMI
KYOTO
ISE
OWARI
Mt Fuji ▲
Nagashima 1573 ✕
Asuke
Okehazama 1560 ✕
MIKAWA
N
Okazaki
SURUGA
Tsukude
IGA
Noda 1573
✕ Nagashino
Ise Bay
TŌTŌMI
Yoshida
0   25 Miles
✕ Mikata ga hara 1572
Mikawa Bay
0   40 Km
Hamamatsu
Takatenjin 1574

	Oda
	Tokugawa
	Takeda
	Uesugi

the military dictators who ruled on behalf of an emperor who since 1185 had been reduced to the position of a figurehead. The Shogunates suffered many vicissitudes during those years. There had been attempts at imperial restoration, conflicts within ruling houses, and one episode of foreign invasion. However, until the mid-15th century the institution of the Shogun, which at that time was vested in successive generations of the Ashikaga family, still managed to control and govern the country.

The tragedy for the Ashikaga happened in 1467, when a civil war, known as the Onin War from the traditional 'year' in which it occurred, began to destroy Kyoto, the capital city of Japan. As the ashes settled the fighting spread further afield, setting in motion sporadic conflicts that were to last for 11 years. Some semblance of order was finally restored, but not before many samurai generals had realised that the Ashikaga Shogunate was gradually losing its power and authority, and that if the samurai wished to increase their land holdings by the use of force against their neighbours, then there was little likelihood of any intervention from the centre to stop them. Thus over the next 50 years Japan slowly split into a number of petty kingdoms, ruled by men who called themselves *daimyô* (great names). Some had held lands in their regions for centuries, and had increased their power by the readiness of neighbours to ally themselves to a powerful protector. Others seized power by murder, intrigue or invasion, and held on to that power by military might.

It would be a mistake to look upon the daimyô of the early 16th century as bandit leaders. In many cases their lands were well governed, and the men who worked in their rice fields, nearly all of whom were part-time soldiers, showed their overlords a degree of loyalty that the Ashikaga Shoguns would have envied. Such loyalty was expressed through willing and enthusiastic military service, carried out on the daimyô's behalf when a call to arms was issued. It was said of the followers of one daimyô, the Chôsokabe of Shikoku Island, that these farmer-samurai were so ready to fight that they tilled the rice-paddies with their spears thrust into the ground at the edge of the field and their sandals tied to the shafts.

As the Sengoku-jidai wore on it was inevitable that smaller daimyô territories should be swallowed by bigger ones, until by about 1560 Japan consisted of a number of major power blocs, alternately in alliance or in conflict as the balance of power shifted from one lord to another. In the midst of it stood the Shogun, impotent in military terms but immensely powerful as a symbol. By ancient convention no one could become Shogun unless he possessed the appropriate lineage back to the original Minamoto family – an honour enjoyed by the Ashikaga. The secret to controlling Japan, therefore, was control of the Shogun.

In 1560 a decisive point was reached when a powerful daimyô called Imagawa Yoshimoto planned to march on Kyoto and set up his own puppet Shogunate. The first obstacle Imagawa had to overcome was a neighbour called Oda Nobunaga, whose much smaller territory was inconveniently situated between Imagawa and his goal. Full of confidence, the Imagawa army moved into Owari province, where they were unexpectedly and thoroughly defeated. Oda Nobunaga launched a surprise attack on them and succeeded in spite of odds of 12 to one against him. This victory, the battle of Okehazama, flung Oda Nobunaga into the big league of daimyô. His military prowess and his convenient

location – not far from the capital – ensured alliances and support, not the least of which was a long-standing association with the ruler of neighbouring Mikawa province, Tokugawa Ieyasu, formerly a retainer of the Imagawa but freed from that obligation by the victory at Okehazama.

For the next 15 years Oda Nobunaga fought battles, made marriage alliances, arranged coups and built castles, until in 1568 he himself was able to enter Kyoto in triumph with Ashikaga Yoshiaki, whom he proclaimed Shogun. More battles and campaigns followed, among which there began a long and bitter struggle between the Oda and the Buddhist fanatics of the Ikkō-ikki, whose well trained fighting men were the equal of any daimyô's army.

In spite of having control of the Shogun, Oda Nobunaga still effectively ruled only a handful of provinces around the capital in central Japan, and some very powerful enemies lay just over the horizon. To the west were the Mori, who controlled the Inland Sea, to the north were the Uesugi, and to the east were the mighty Takeda, under their daimyô, Takeda Shingen.

The Takeda Clan

Of all the daimyô who had the potential to rule Japan, Takeda Shingen had demonstrated his ability most clearly by his own successful hegemony in Kai and Shinano provinces. Three factors had prevented him from taking the same initiative of marching on Kyoto as had been exercised by Imagawa Yoshimoto in 1560. The first was the isolation of his mountain-based province from the central area. The second was the fact that any advance by Shingen down towards the Tokaido, the road which ran along the Pacific coast, was monitored and blocked by Oda Nobunaga's allies the Tokugawa. Finally, for much of his reign Takeda Shingen was occupied in fighting his enemies to the north and east of his own territory, in particular the Hôjô family, based near modern Tokyo, and the Uesugi, whom he contested on five occasions at the same place – the battlefield of Kawanakajima.

In the winter of 1572 Takeda Shingen broke out of his territories and made a move towards the Pacific coast. He threatened the Tokugawa in Hamamatsu castle and then defeated them when Tokugawa Ieyasu led his army out to fight him on the plain of Mikata-ga-hara. It proved to be an indecisive victory because the winter weather prevented any follow-up, but the defeat of the Tokugawa encouraged Takeda Shingen to return the following year. This time he laid siege to Tokugawa Ieyasu's castle of Noda, on the Toyokawa river. The garrison were soon driven to the point of surrender, but, according to legend, had in their castle a large stock of *sake* (rice wine). Not wishing to allow this precious brew to fall into the hands of the enemy, the defenders of Noda decided to dispose of it in the most appropriate manner. The sounds of the party reached the besiegers' ears, and Takeda Shingen was particularly taken by the music of a bamboo flute being played on the ramparts. He moved forward to hear the tune more clearly and was spotted by a sniper on the

castle walls who put a bullet through his head. Takeda Shingen died a few days later, living just long enough to urge his followers to keep his death secret for as long as possible, as so much of the formidable reputation of the Takeda army rested on his own broad shoulders.

Takeda Shingen was succeeded by his son Takeda Katsuyori, who inherited the mantle of the all-conquering Takeda daimyô and the considerable military experience of the fine Takeda army with its renowned cavalry force. It was not long before he decided to follow in his father's footsteps by invading the territories of Tokugawa Ieyasu. He set off in 1575, but his route was different from the ones which Takeda Shingen had followed. Instead Takeda Katsuyori headed straight for the Tokugawa capital of Okazaki in Mikawa province because he had been reliably informed that a traitor there was willing to open the gates for them. However, while Takeda Katsuyori was still on his way the traitor was relieved of his head, leaving the invading army bereft of its primary target as they had insufficient strength to take Okazaki unaided. Katsuyori was forced to change his plans, and decided to capture a smaller castle as compensation. He therefore took a different road back from Mikawa, one which followed the long flat plain along the Toyokawa from the sea and up into the mountains. The road was defended by three castles. The nearest one was Yoshida, where the Toyokawa entered the sea. Yoshida withstood Katsuyori's attack, so he turned his attentions to the point where the flat plain ended and the security of the mountains began. Here, on the edge of a cliff, lay a tiny fortress called Nagashino.

CHRONOLOGY

1560   Battle of Okehazama. Oda Nobunaga defeats and kills
Imagawa Yoshimoto.

1571   Oda Nobunaga burns Enryakuji.

1572   Takeda Shingen defeats Tokugawa Ieyasu at the battle of Mikata-ga-hara.

1575   **5 April:** Okudaira Sadamasa appointed keeper of Nagashino.
29 May: Takeda Katsuyori visits the shrine of Shingen.
30 May: The Takeda army leaves Kofu.
13 June: Takeda Katsuyori burns Nirengi and Ushikubo and attacks
Yoshida.
14 June: Katsuyori leaves Yoshida.
16 June: Takeda Katsuyori arrives at Nagashino.
17-21 June: Four days of continual attacks on the castle.
22 June: Nagashino garrison loses the storehouse. The Takeda begin a
blockade.
Conference of Oda and Tokugawa at Okazaki.
25 June: Oda and Tokugawa armies leave Okazaki.
26 June: Oda and Tokugawa armies reach Noda.
27 June: Fences built, both armies prepare.
28 June: Battle of Nagashino.

1582   Takeda Katsuori finally defeated, extinction of the Takeda family.
Murder of Oda Nobunaga by one of his generals, he is succeeded by
Toyotomi Hideyoshi.

1582   Battle of Komaki-Nagakute. Hideyoshi and Ieyasu fight to a standstill.
Ieyasu later allies himself with Hideyoshi

1590   Hideyoshi virtually completes subjugation of Japan.

1598   Death of Hideyoshi.

1600   Battle of Sekigahara.

1603   Tokugawa Ieyasu becomes Shogun.

OPPOSING COMMANDERS

Takeda Katsuyori

It is no enviable task to inherit the reputation of a father who has become a legend in his own lifetime, yet this was the burden placed on the shoulders of Takeda Katsuyori following the death of Shingen in 1573. Takeda Katsuyori was born in 1546, at the time when Takeda Shingen was expanding his territories from Kai into Shinano province. In 1544 Shingen had defeated in battle a local daimyô called Suwa Yorishige and then forced Yorishige to commit suicide following a humiliating and spurious peace conference. Yorishige had a 14-year-old daughter of great beauty, whose mother was Shingen's younger sister. She had witnessed the defeat of her family and the judicial murder of her father at the hands of the Takeda, but then had had to suffer a personal anguish because Shingen became infatuated with her and took her – his own niece – to be one of his wives.

Takeda Shingen was so obsessed with the girl that his superstitious followers became alarmed and believed her to be an incarnation of the white fox-spirit of the Suwa Shrine, who had bewitched him in order to gain revenge. A fox assuming the form of a beautiful woman and making a man fall in love with her is a popular theme in Japanese folk belief. This 'fox lady' gave birth to Katsuyori in 1546 and died when her son was nine, so that when the destruction of the house came about through Katsuyori, wise old heads nodded, remembering the unhappy circumstances of his birth and the rumours about his magical mother.

As Shingen had doted on his mother, so he made Katsuyori his favourite son, to the extent of bestowing on him the character 'Yori' in his name, which was common in the Suwa family, rather than 'Nobu', which he bore himself (as Harunobu) and which his other sons also used. This always set him aside as rather special, and he became heir after the death in 1567 of his elder brother Yoshinobu.

Katsuyori was nonetheless a capable leader of samurai. He was schooled in the Takeda tradition of mobile warfare and knew how to handle the considerable striking force of the Takeda horsemen. He had fought well at Kawanakajima and had played a valuable part in the Battle of Mikata-ga-Hara, but when he succeeded his father he soon made enemies among Shingen's old retainers. The ageing generals had considerable respect for Katsuyori as a soldier, but little else. These men, the surviving members of Takeda Shingen's 'Twenty-Four Generals', possessed a wealth of experience in matters both military and political which they were more than willing to share with their new heir. However, Katsuyori proved unwilling to listen to their recommendations, preferring to make major policy decisions without undertaking any consultation with this key group of advisers. They had urged a defensive and consolidatory strategy following Shingen's death, but this advice was

A print depicting Takeda Katsuyori, who, in spite of all his earlier achievements, has gone down in history as the commander who was defeated at the battle of Nagashino. Katsuyori lived under the considerable shadow of his late father Takeda Shingen, and it may well have been a desire to emulate his father's achievements that led to the campaign and battle of Nagashino.

completely ignored. As a result, the decisive move by Katsuyori to invade Mikawa province was taken against the recommendation of the men who had to follow him into action.

Oda Nobunaga

Like the Takeda, Oda Nobunaga was served by a handful of very able generals, but in his case there was considerable mutual respect. By the time of the battle of Nagashino Oda Nobunaga had become established as one of the finest leaders of samurai that Japan had ever seen. He had been born in 1534, and had inherited his father's domains at the age of 15. He was bold and resourceful, and had the ability that was lacking in Takeda Katsuyori to benefit from the advice and experience of others. He had learned this the hard way when one of his retainers committed suicide in protest at the young lord's earlier attitude. The battle of Okehazama showed his military genius. This victory over the Imagawa had come about through an appreciation of a military situation and a rapid response. Reliable intelligence had come to him that the Imagawa army was resting in a narrow gorge and celebrating the fall of one of Nobunaga's castles. Realising that they would be off guard Oda Nobunaga led his men round in a surprise attack and took advantage of a sudden thunderstorm. His subsequent victories showed the same combination of careful planning and rapid execution, but he was also wise enough to realise that he did not have the power to defeat major enemies acting alone. The battle of the Anegawa, in 1570, although planned and controlled by Oda Nobunaga, depended for victory on his allies the Tokugawa.

Oda Nobunaga also possessed a great streak of ruthlessness. Frustrated by his inability to crush the militant Buddhist peasant armies of the Ikkô-ikki, Nobunaga demonstrated his force to them by destroying a soft target, the ancient monastic complex of Mount Hiei, near Kyoto, whose 'warrior monks' had supported the Ikkô-ikki. Tens of thousands of people were slaughtered and the entire monastery was burned. Ironically, Nobunaga owed the monastic armies a great debt of gratitude, for it was they who had taught him to be flexible in his fighting techniques. Nobunaga's great strength was an appreciation of the most effective way in which firearms could be used, a lesson he had learned at the hands of the Ikkô-ikki. His position at the centre of power in Japan also enabled him to be at the forefront of military technology, and his links with Portuguese traders and his tolerance of Christianity gave him better access to European military hardware than many of his contemporaries, including the Takeda.

Tokugawa Ieyasu

Oda Nobunaga's ally Tokugawa Ieyasu, who was born in 1542, had learned the virtues of patience and loyalty through long years as a hostage of the Imagawa family. The death of Imagawa Yoshimoto released him from this burden, and he began applying himself to consolidating and defending his territory of Mikawa province, to which he eventually added neighbouring Tôtômi. By the time of the battle of Nagashino Ieyasu had matured from a spirited and sometimes reckless leader of samurai to a careful and intelligent general. At the battle of Azukizaka, in 1564, he had led his followers into battle, receiving spear cuts and bullet wounds. By

Oda Nobunaga, from a painted hanging scroll in the Okumura mansion, Inuyama. The battle of Nagashino in 1575 is Nobunaga's greatest victory. It was a triumph both for his skills as a general, and his ability to learn from previous mistakes. His experience from the long campaign against the monk fanatics of the Ikkô-ikki at Nagashima and the battle of Mikata-ga-hara in 1572 are both evident in the approach he took to the challenge of the Takeda cavalry at Nagashino.

1570, at the battle of the Anegawa, he was controlling the Tokugawa army through a well organised battlefield communication system and was defended by a devoted bodyguard unit.

In 1572 Ieyasu narrowly avoided a crushing defeat when the Takeda invaded his territories and fought him at Mikata-ga-hara. The return of the Takeda in 1575, led by Takeda Katsuyori, placed Ieyasu once more in the firing line. Here his diplomatic skills in securing the continued support of Oda Nobunaga, who was not directly threatened by Katsuyori, proved as important as his military ones. All in all at Nagashino, Tokugawa Ieyasu was to show the qualities of generalship, diplomacy and good judgement which were ultimately to give him the supreme prize in Japan when he was proclaimed Shogun in 1603.

Okudaira Sadamasa

Nagashino castle was defended against the Takeda assault by Okudaira Sadamasa (1555-1615), a very capable soldier who was familiar with the territory and supported by a loyal and equally brave garrison. His appointment to the post was itself a challenge to Takeda Katsuyori. The Okudaira were a Mikawa family and were originally retainers of the Tokugawa, but had been forced to join Takeda Shingen. The Takeda can never have been very sure of their loyalty, because Sadamasa's wife and younger brother were kept as permanent hostages in the Takeda headquarters in Kofu – hostage-taking, which was often done voluntarily as a means of assuring one's loyalty to the overlord, was a very common arrangement in 16th century Japan.

With the death of Shingen in 1573, Okudaira Sadamasa decided to rejoin the Tokugawa, and marched his men out of the castle of Tsukude, which they had garrisoned on behalf of the Takeda. When news of this betrayal reached Takeda Katsuyori, he had Sadamasa's family crucified. The result was to make the Okudaira into bitter enemies of Takeda Katsuyori, and when Tokugawa Ieyasu was looking for a retainer to place in charge of the strategic castle of Nagashino, which controlled movements into Mikawa from the Takeda territories, the appointment of Okudaira Sadamasa was a guarantee of determined resistance should the two sides ever meet in conflict.

Tokugawa Ieyasu, as depicted on a painted scroll in the Nagashino Castle Preservation Hall. The Tokugawa held a strategic position between Oda Nobunaga and Takeda Katsuyori, and it was a raid by the Takeda on to the Tokugawa territories that precipitated the siege and battle of Nagashino. The Okudaira family, who defended Nagashino, were retainers of the Tokugawa who had once been forced to fight for the Takeda.

OPPOSING ARMIES

This is a typical suit of armour of the Sengoku Period, such as would have been seen at many battles around the time of Nagashino. The breastplate is made of horizontal layers of iron riveted together, while the *kusazuri* (tassets) are of conventional *kebiki-odoshi* (close-spaced lacing). Note the two straightforward *kote* (shoulder plates) and the simple *kote* (sleeve armour).

The Structure of a Samurai Army

At the battle of Nagashino both sides commanded armies that were broadly similar in a number of aspects, yet had differences that were to prove crucial in the battle itself. The similarities that existed among most samurai armies had arisen from competition, so that the typical samurai army had evolved into an efficient fighting machine that possessed certain basic features. The first characteristic was a recognised structure of feudal obligation that the daimyô could transform with the minimum of effort into an army. The most important resources of fighting men came from within the daimyô's own extended family and from among the families who were hereditary vassals, called the *fudai*. Next, and less reliable, were contingents supplied from neighbouring territories, such as those of a vanquished enemy. Finally, there would be allied armies who would join a daimyô's army for a variety of reasons, usually self-interest.

The numbers of troops supplied by these different sources varied greatly in quality and quantity. The wealth of a landowner, or a fief-holder, was expressed in *koku*, one koku being the amount of rice thought necessary to feed one man for one year. Feudal obligation required the supply of troops according to wealth. As a rule of thumb two mounted men and 20 foot per 1,000 koku would be supplied, although the proportion varied enormously from year to year and from daimyô to daimyô. By such means the commander could assemble a host whose numbers, strength and weaponry were calculable in advance.

The elite of the daimyô's army were the samurai themselves. The word 'samurai', which is nowadays taken to mean any Japanese fighting man, had a narrower definition during the Sengoku period. At that time the samurai were the knightly class who rode horses. Mounted warriors had always been an elite in Japan. The first samurai had been mounted archers, and their armour, though not unduly heavy, provided the protection they had needed as mobile 'gun platforms'. Early samurai warfare was a matter of archery duels, concluded with sidearms, against a worthy opponent who was also of samurai rank. The samurai were attended by an equal number of lower-ranking soldiers who fought on foot and had as their primary role the support of their master rather than direct combat.

Samurai Arms and Armour

By the Sengoku-jidai there had been considerable changes in the make-up of a samurai army. Many poorer samurai either could not afford horses sor simply chose to fight on foot, and the daimyô had also realised that to augment and hold their territories they had to rely increasingly on the services of lower ranking, lower class footsoldiers. This change became apparent in the weaponry of the samurai. Exclusive use of the

A section of armour plate laced in the *sugake-odoshi* (spaced out lacing) style. The individual scales are of lacquered iron. The *sugake* style had the convenience of being quicker to make than the *kebiki* style, while losing none of its flexibility, and much armour of the time of Nagashino would have been made like this.

bow had laid the mounted samurai open to attack from bands of footsoldiers, so in time the bow was abandoned in favour of the long, straight spear, which enabled the samurai to defend himself and take the fight to the enemy in a way that the bow had not allowed. He was still attended by a group of followers, who could hand to him a bow or spear as required, but chronicles of the time and contemporary illustrations clearly show that the spear became the preferred weapon on the battlefield. When Shimazu Toyohisa rode into battle at Sekigahara in 1600 carrying a bow it was thought sufficiently unusual for the chronicler to make particular note of it.

Most illustrations show mounted samurai spearmen wearing a rounded style of armour called a *dô-maru* instead of the older box-like *yoroi*, to which the addition of a solid breastplate was practically the only major change in design during the whole of the 'Warring States Period'. Armour was worn on the sleeves, arms, legs and face, with a *sashimono* – an identifying device, frequently a flag – worn on the back of the samurai's armour. Troops from a particular unit would wear identical sashimonos.

The type of spear the samurai carried was called a *mochi-yari* (held spear). The shaft length varied between 3.2m and 4m, and blade lengths varied considerably between about 10cm and 1.5m. Techniques were developed to enable the samurai to use this weapon in any situation: from a horse, in a charge on foot, or to defend castle walls. Some illustrations suggest that the spears were used as lances from the saddle, others that they were more used for slashing strokes while standing up in the stirrups. No daimyô army was better skilled at the use of mounted troops than the Takeda. The victories of Ueda, in 1548, and Mikata-ga-hara, in 1572, owed a great deal to the mobile and hard-hitting power of the devastating Takeda cavalry charge.

The Ashigaru

The footsoldiers at whom the cavalry charged were no disorganised rabble, for the daimyô realised that for footsoldiers to be of any use

A samurai body armour of solid plate construction is shown here folded out to illustrate how the five parts fit together. The kusazuri would be suspended from a row of holes around the lower edges. The ties that hold the armour together around the samurai's body are found under the right armpit. The prominent bracket is to hold the pole of the *sashimono*, the identifying device (usually a flag) that was worn on the back of the armour.

against samurai they had to be trained and disciplined. The original name for them – *ashigaru* (light feet) – changed from meaning a haphazard bunch of absconded peasants to what were effectively the 'other ranks' of the samurai class. The new respect for the ashigaru was shown by the practice of dressing them in uniform armour and colours. Yamagata Masakage, who fought for the Takeda at Nagashino, dressed all his army, including the ashigaru, in red-lacquered armour, yet even this apparent uniformity concealed a certain amount of rank distinction, for close examination would have revealed that the ashigaru armour was not of the quality worn by the higher ranks of samurai. It was frequently of simple construction, with the commander's personal *mon* (badge) lacquered on to the front. Armoured sleeves might be included, but the ashigaru was unlikely to sport the *haidate* (thigh guards) or *suneate* (shin guards) of his betters. The biggest difference in appearance and protection, however, came with the helmet. In place of the samurai's *kabuto* (helmet) and face-mask, the ashigaru wore a simple iron *jingasa* (war hat), which was usually shaped like a lampshade and had a cloth neckguard hanging from the rear.

A simple face mask. One of the most noticeable innovations in Japanese armour during the 16th century was the introduction of armour for the face. It commonly fitted to just below the eyes, as shown in this example, which has a removable nosepiece. The two projecting bolts under the cheeks are there to take the cords which tied the helmet on to the head. Some later examples sported whiskers made of horsehair.

The role of the footsoldier as warrior's assistant continued, and as many as 40 per cent of the total number of troops in a typical army could be ashigaru performing simple but vital support functions such as baggage carriers, grooms and drummers. The remainder of the ashigaru force would be organised in corps of specialised weaponry: bows, spears and matchlock guns. Archers were the least in number, since prowess with the bow required years of practice as well as muscular strength. The ashigaru archers were therefore highly trained sharp-shooters, and were often employed as skirmishers. In addition, along with the matchlockmen, they could form lines of missile troops, supplied with a large number of arrows carried in 100-arrow box quivers. Archers sometimes appear to be regarded as the least important of the three arms, and in the 1575 Uesugi muster rolls they are included within the 'other troops' category (total 1,018), alongside 3,609 spearmen, 321 matchlockmen and 566 mounted samurai.

Spearmen were usually the largest category. Oda Nobunaga was probably the first to introduce disciplined ashigaru spear units into his army and he possessed a contingent who made up 27 per cent of his fighting force. The longest spears of all were also to be found in the Oda armies, with a giant 5.6m shaft. It seems that Nobunaga adopted them quite early on in his career, because there is a reference in the *Shinchôkoki* dated April 1553 to '500 three and a half *ken* [5.6m] long spears'. These *nagae-yari* (long-shafted spears) were probably used like pikes. Some form of 'pike drill' must have taken place, and there is evidence from contemporary illustrations of the ashigaru pikemen forming a hedge behind the matchlockmen to protect them. All the ashigaru units were under the command of an *ashigaru-taishô* (ashigaru general), which implies a high degree of discipline. Unfortunately, in the accounts of the wars, it is the lowest ranking soldiers who get forgotten, and descriptions of ashigaru warfare tend to appear as anonymous groups of weaponry. A samurai may be recorded as 'falling prey to the ranks of spearmen', or being 'laid low in a hail of gunfire', but further details of actual use have to be inferred.

A samurai holding a spear, with the support for a sashimono clearly visible on the back of his armour. Regardless of the prestige and lore associated with the Japanese samurai sword, a spear was the preferred primary fighting weapon on the battlefields of 16th century Japan. The spear was skilfully wielded from horseback, but was also employed on foot and in sieges. The armour in this photograph is of *nuinobe-do* style, and is decorated on the edges with black fur.

The Arquebus Corps

Both the Takeda and Oda armies possessed firearms, and since their use by the Oda was to prove decisive, a brief discussion is needed about these weapons and how they were used prior to Nagashino. Simple Chinese handguns had been known in Japan since 1510, and in 1543 they were joined by more sophisticated Portuguese models. The island on which the Portuguese landed was owned by the Shimazu clan, and it was to Shimazu Takahisa that the honour went of conducting the first battle in Japanese history where the new firearms were used. This was in his attack on the fortress of Kajiki, in Osumi province, in 1549. He was one of several warlords to appreciate the potential shown by these new weapons, and local swordsmiths, who were already renowned for their metal-working skills, applied themselves to learning how to copy the arquebuses and then to mass produce them. Connections with Portuguese traders also proved very important, and it is no coincidence that the first Christian converts among the samurai class became regular users of arquebuses. Oda Nobunaga's support for Christian missionaries was a great help in this regard.

The Portuguese arquebus was a simple but well designed weapon. Unlike the heavier type of muskets which required a rest, the arquebus could be fired from the shoulder, with support needed only for the heavier calibre versions which the Japanese later developed – usually known as 'wall guns' or 'hand cannon'. In a normal arquebus an iron barrel fitted neatly into a wooden stock. To the right of the stock was a brass serpentine linked to a spring which dropped the serpentine when the trigger was pulled. The serpentine contained the end of a glowing and smouldering match, the rest of which was wrapped around the stock of the gun, or wound around the gunner's arm. Arquebuses are therefore often called simply 'matchlocks'. To prevent premature explosions, the pan, into which the fine priming gunpowder had been carefully introduced, was closed by a brass sliding cover which swung back at the last moment. The guns produced quite a recoil and a lot of smoke, as shown in the annual festival at Nagashino, where reproduction matchlocks are fired. As time went by cartridges were introduced, thus speeding up the process of loading.

A Portuguese adventurer wrote that within two or three years the Japanese had succeeded in making several hundred guns, and by the 1550s they were regularly seen in action in battle. The best gunsmiths

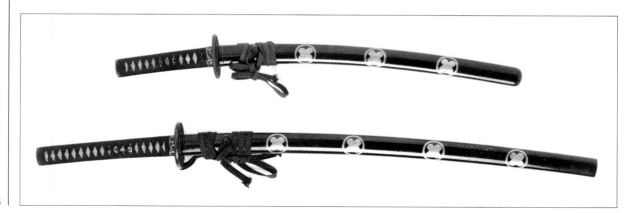

A quick way of getting into a suit of armour was by supporting the body armour, to which the sleeves had already been attached, from the ceiling with a rope. The samurai then clambered in. He is already wearing his *haidate* (thighguards) and his *waraji* (straw sandals), so he will be soon ready for battle.

OPPOSITE The classic *daisho* (pair of swords) that was the badge of the samurai class. The longer was called a *katana*, and the shorter was known as the *wakizashi*. In armour the katana alone would be worn, slung from a scabbard-carrier attached to the belt, where it would be accompanied by a *tanto* (dagger). By the end of the 16th century the Japanese sword had acquired the mystique it still enjoys today, and fine specimens were highly prized and very expensive.

formed schools to pass on the tradition, such as those at Kunitomo and Sakai, and were never short of customers. Within the space of a few years arquebuses were being produced to quality standards that exceeded those originally brought from Europe. One simple, yet fundamental, development which occurred quite early on in Japanese arquebus production was the standardisation of the bore. In Europe, where no form of standardisation was carried out, practically every gun needed its own bullet mould. In Japan, bores were standardised to a handful of sizes. Standard bores meant standard sized bullets which could be carried in bulk for an arquebus corps – a small, but significant improvement in production and use.

In 1549 Oda Nobunaga placed an order for 500 arquebuses with the gunsmiths of Kunitomo. In 1555 Takeda Shingen used 300 in an attack on a castle owned by Uesugi Kenshin and was so impressed that he placed 500 arquebuses in one of his own castles. However, few daimyô appreciated that the successful employment of firearms depended only partly on technical matters such as accuracy of fire and speed of loading. Just as was the case in Europe then, in the time it took to fire a succession of arquebus balls a skilled archer could launch many more arrows, and with considerably more accuracy. On the other hand, to use a bow properly required an elite archer corps, but the arquebus could be mastered in a comparatively short time, making it the ideal weapon for the lower ranking ashigaru.

The secret to success with firearms was therefore the same as the secret of success with any infantry unit: good army organisation and a considerable change in social attitudes. To achieve this there first had to be a recognition that the ashigaru could be more than a casually recruited rabble, and a commitment had to be given to their training and welfare. This had been achieved by both the Takeda and the Oda prior to 1575, but it took a further leap of the imagination to give them pride of place in a samurai army, because traditionally the vanguard of an army had always consisted of the most experienced and trusted swordsmen and mounted samurai. Yet for firearms to be effective they had to be placed in the front ranks in large numbers. All that was needed was a demonstration of how successful this method could be.

Oda Nobunaga had already used a volley-firing technique at Mureki in 1554. It had also been used against him by the Buddhist fanatics of the Ikkô-ikki at their fortress cathedral of Ishiyama Hongan-ji, built where Osaka castle now stands. Nobunaga's first move against the Ishiyama Hongan-ji was launched in August 1570. He had established a series of forts around it, but on 12 September the bells rang out at midnight from within the Ishiyama Hongan-ji and two of Nobunaga's fortresses were attacked. The Oda army were stunned both by the ferocity of the surprise attack and by the use of controlled volley firing from 3,000 matchlock men. This little known battle pre-dates Nagashino by five years and was probably the first example of large scale organised volleyed musket fire used in battle in Japan. In the chronicle *Shinchôkoki* we read that the enemy gunfire 'echoed between heaven and earth', resulting in the withdrawal of the Oda main body, leaving a handful of forts to attempt the task of monitoring, if not controlling, the mighty fortress of Ishiyama Hongan-ji – a process that would take 11 years and much of Nobunaga's military resources.

This encounter provided an excellent demonstration of how matchlocks might best be employed, and it is surely no coincidence that it came from the Ikkô-ikki. Being composed largely of lower class troops, their mere existence proved the power of well organised ashigaru armies, and their use of firearms was simply one very dramatic way of expressing it. Lacking any of the social constraints likely to impede a samurai's appreciation of the potential combination of ashigaru and guns, the monk armies simply adopted a new weapon on military grounds alone. Showing the ability to learn from experience that was to mark his career, Oda Nobunaga put his own arquebuses into action against the Ikkô-ikki fortress of Nagashima in 1573. Copying the monks' techniques, Nobunaga hoped that concentrated arquebus fire would blast a way into the fortress for him. However, the defenders were saved by a sudden downpour which soaked the matches of the Oda guns, rendering nine out of ten non-fireable, and the attack failed. This was another military lesson not to be lost on Oda Nobunaga.

The Samurai Army on the Battlefield

Any Sengoku battle tended to be fought between alliances of clan armies, set out according to an agreed battle plan and co-ordinated through the mobile *tsukai-ban* (messengers). Each clan army was further subdivided into weapon groups, and co-ordinated through its own band of tsukai. Within each army fought high-ranking mounted samurai spearmen who each supplied a handful of personal retainers according to their means. Other samurai retainers fought on foot with spears, supported by ashigaru. Specialised corps of highly trained ashigaru wielded bows or arquebuses, and all were under the command of officers. A sizeable support unit was included in each army. Flag bearers were the most important element of this unit and had their own guard. Within each clan army there would be a large headquarters unit who formed the lord's bodyguard. Careful strategic planning, with the co-operation between separate clan armies facilitated by a skilled battlefield communication system, enabled a successful commander to control synchronised movement by units who were physically separated, with each man knowing his role in the endeavour. Both Oda Nobunaga and Takeda Shingen possessed sufficient resources to support such a model by supplying and training their armies. This ensured the continuing loyalty of their men.

THE ARMY OF ODA NOBUNAGA

The overall number of troops in the conflict was as follows:

Oda Nobunaga	30,000
Tokugawa Ieyasu	8,000
Okudaira Sadamasa (the Nagashino garrison)	500
Takeda Katsuyori	15,000

Oda Nobunaga, who was then the strongest daimyô in all Japan, had a total army of 100,000, from which he committed 30,000 (30 per cent) to the relief of Nagashino. Many of the others were still actively engaged in

ABOVE **A miniature arquebus, showing details of the touch hole and serpentine. The touch hole is covered by a hinged brass cover to guard against premature explosions. The smouldering match would fit into the end of the serpentine, and the ramrod slid under the barrel. This example bears the *mon* (badge) of the Tokugawa on top of the barrel.**

the long war with the Ikkô-ikki. The contingents present at Nagashino were organised along a pattern common to all daimyô – of relatives, vassals and others. The names of the leaders who appear under the various categories are as follows:

Ichizoku-shû (the family corps)
Oda Nobutada (1557-1582) (the eldest son of Nobunaga)
Oda Nobuo (1558-1630)
(Nobunaga's second son, adopted into the Kitabatake family in 1569)

Go-umamawari-shû (bodyguard)
The bodyguard contained the elite of Nobunaga's army and was divided into three separate units:

1. Hashiba Hideyoshi – a unit commanded by Nobunaga's ablest general, later to be known as Toyotomi Hideyoshi, the man who would succeed in unifying Japan.
2. Kuro *horô-shû* (the black *horô* unit). A horô was a stiffened cloak worn on the back of armour by mounted men in place of the more usual flag sashimono. It was given a rounded shape by being stretched over a light bamboo framework. The men of the black horô unit present at Nagashino were Kawajiri Hidetaka, Sasa Narimasa and Nogamura Sanjurô.
3. Aka *horô-shû* (the red horô unit). Five of this elite corps took part in the battle: Maeda Toshiie, Mori Kawachi-no-kami, Kanamori Nagachika, Fukutomi Hiraza'emon and Harada Naomasa. The members of both horô-shû would have had a few attendants each but no other troops, since at Nagashino they were placed in charge of the matchlockmen.

Fudai-shû (hereditary vassals)
Niwa Nagahide
Sakuma Nobumori
Shibata Katsuie

Tozama-shû (the 'outer lords')
Takigawa Kazumasu
Nagaoka Fujitaka
Akechi Mitsuhide
Andô Noritoshi
Mori Yoshinari

Unfortunately the numbers of each contingent are not known. The Oda army had 3,500 matchlocks, all of which were taken to Nagashino. Five hundred were sent on the dawn raid on Tobigasuyama, leaving 3,000 to face the Takeda cavalry.

LEFT **A mounted samurai, adorned with severed head trophies. Since ancient times the one sure proof that a samurai had done his duty was by the presentation to his lord of the heads of his defeated enemies. This warrior has a fine collection of four heads in all, one of which is still stuck on his spear blade. He has slung his helmet over his shoulder, and is wearing the samurai's *jinbaori*, a form of sleeveless surcoat. Arrows are protruding from his armour.**

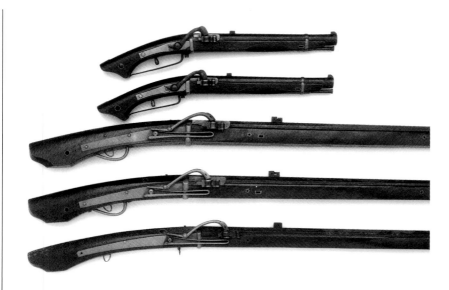

THE TOKUGAWA ARMY

Tokugawa Ieyasu supplied 8,000 men out of his total of 12,500, which was 64 per cent – a large commitment of resources as they were his territories that were being attacked. As many of his other troops were holding castles that were also under threat from the Takeda, almost the entire Tokugawa army was engaged in some way or another in the struggle with Katsuyori. The Tokugawa structure resembled that of the Oda. The relatives and fudai appeared in two units, one for western Mikawa province, the other for eastern Mikawa. Commanders present at Nagashino were as follows:

Under Ishikawa Kazumasa (commander of western Mikawa)
Matsudaira Kiyomune
Matsudaira Nobukazu
Matsudaira Tadatsugu
Naitô Ienaga
Hiraiwa Chikayoshi

Under Sakai Tadatsugu (commander of eastern Mikawa)
Matsudaira Tadamasa
Matsudaira Ietada
Honda Hirotaka
Nishikyô Iekazu
Okudaira Tadayoshi
Suganuma Sadamitsu

***Hatamoto* (headquarters troops)**
Honda Tadakatsu
Sakakibara Yasumasa
Okubo Tadayo
Torii Mototada
plus others.

Again, no numbers are available for individual commanders.

THE TAKEDA ARMY

It is possible to be much more precise about the composition of the Takeda army at Nagashino. The great chronicle of the Takeda, the *Kôyô Gunkan*, contains a very detailed breakdown of the clan army during the time of Shingen. Each named individual is listed along with the number of horsemen he supplied to the Takeda army, and it is unlikely that these numbers changed at all with the succession of Katsuyori. Since there are very good records of the names of samurai leaders present at Nagashino, it is a straightforward task to look each one up in the *Kôyô Gunkan* and thus compute the size and make-up of the Takeda force. To do this I have used the list in Futaki's book *Nagashino no tatakai* and added the number of horsemen from the *Kôyô Gunkan*. The sub-divisions of the army are similar to that of the Oda and Tokugawa, and consisted of three overall parts: *jikishindan*, *sakikata-shû* and *kuni-shû*. The kuni-shû (provincial corps), levies from the villages, were not represented at Nagashino. Of the others, those present at Nagashino are listed as follows under the commanders' names. Further biographical details of the commanders themselves appear in a later chapter. In several cases only the surnames are known.

The jikishindan (the 'close retainer' group) was subdivided into four:

1. *Goshinrui-shû* (relatives group)

Anayama Nobukimi	200
Ichijô Nobutatsu	200
Takeda Nobukado	80
Takeda Nobumitsu	100
Takeda Nobutoyo	200
Takeda Nobutomo (presumably in a personal capacity only)	0
Takeda Nobuzane	15
Takeda Katsuyori (his personal force)	200
Mochizuki Nobumasa	60

Each of the above horsemen would have worn the Takeda mon on their sashimono, while the leader's personal banner would have had its own device.

2. *Go fudai karo-shû* (fudai and elders)

Atobe Katsusuke	300
Amari Nobuyasu	100
Oyamada Masayuki	70
Oyamada Nobushige	200
Kosaka Masazumi	20
Tsuchiya Masatsugu	100
Naitô Masatoyo	250
Hara Masatane	120
Baba Nobuharu	120
Yamagata Masakage	300

These men fought under their leader's personal banner rather than the Takeda mon.

3. Ashigaru-taishô (generals of ashigaru units)

Obata Matagorô	3 (+10 ashigaru)
Obata Nobuhide	12 (+65 ashigaru)
Saigusa Moritomo	30 (+70 ashigaru)
Saigusa Ujimitsu	3 (+10 ashigaru)
Shimosone Masamoto	20 (+50 ashigaru)
Tada Jiro`emon	0 (+10 ashigaru)
Nagasaka Juza`emon	40 (+45 ashigaru)
Yokota Yasukage	30 (+100 ashigaru)

4. *Hatamoto-shoyakunin* (bodyguard and servants) - see below

5. *Sakikata-shû*

The sakikata-shû (the 'companions group') consisted of men supplied by the leaders of the provinces that had been made Takeda fiefs following conquest. All had proved their loyalty thus far by good service. They are listed by province:

SHINANO PROVINCE

Sanada Nobutsuna	200
Sanada Masateru	50
Imogawa Ennosuke	60
Tokita Tosho	10
Matsuoka Ukyô	50
Muroga Nobutoshi	20
Unnamed	60

WESTERN KOZUKE PROVINCE

Obata Nobusada	500
Annaka Kageshige	150
Wada Narimori	30
Unnamed	14

SURUGA PROVINCE

Asahina Nobuoki	150
Okabe Mastsuna	50
Okabe Unsei	10
Unnamed	9

TÔTÔMI AND MIKAWA PROVINCES

Suganuma Sadanao	40
Others	3

ABOVE **Three ashigaru holding spears. The most important weapon groups of ashigaru were guns, spears and bows. The two jingasa being worn here are of different styles. That on the viewer's left is the usual conical design, while that on the right has a curved brim, and is known as the shingen style, after Takeda Shingen. This shape was worn during the Edo period by officials of the Shogun, and were made of lacquered papier-mâché. The ashigaru wear simple *okegawa-dô* armours.**

Kôsaka Masazumi, of the fudai karo-shû is allocated a notional 20 horsemen because at the time of the departure of the Mikawa invasion, Kôsaka Danjô Masanobu, one of the Takeda's most illustrious generals, was already in arms against Uesugi Kenshin, accompanied by an army of 10,000. Presumably that included his own 450 horsemen. Two Kôsakas – Sukenobu and Masazumi – fought at Nagashino, and both were killed, but there is no separate record of horsemen under their names.

The total of all horsemen supplied in the army that went to Nagashino is 4,199, to which we must add the 55 named individuals above (some families supplied two or three as commanders). This brings

the total to 4,254. The total for all the horsemen in the Takeda army in the *Kôyô Gunkan* list is 9,121, which means that the Nagashino force was 47 per cent of the total mounted Takeda army.

Turning to the composition of the complete army, every horseman would have been accompanied by two followers on foot. Takeda Shingen had a personal retinue of 884 ashigaru and servants, who made up the hatamoto-shoyakunin. To this were added various notable samurai from the list above as a bodyguard.

It seems reasonable to assume the same numbers for Katsuyori, and there were, in addition, 5,489 other ashigaru under the command of the other leaders, including the ashigaru-taishô's own command. These figures would give a full Takeda army of 33,736, as follows:

Horsemen	9,121
Two followers each	18,242
Ashigaru in the hatamoto-shoyakunin	884
Other ashigaru	5,489
Total	**33,736**

Since we have established that 47 per cent of the Takeda army took part at Nagashino it seems not unreasonable to apply the same percentage to the figures for ashigaru, including the bodyguard unit, as presumably some would stay behind to guard Katsuyori's family in the headquarters in Kofu. The Nagashino army therefore becomes 15,757 men, distributed as follows:

Horsemen	4,254
Two followers each	8,508
Ashigaru in the hatamoto-shoyakunin	415
Other ashigaru	2,580
Total	**15,757**

This number tallies well with accounts of the battle, which have the army at about 15,000. The deployment of just under half the Takeda army reflects their need to conduct a campaign against the Uesugi at the same time. It also points to the initial aim of Takeda Katsuyori, which was to capture Okazaki in a rapid raid using the treachery of a Tokugawa official.

The figures show that 27 per cent of the Takeda army at Nagashino were mounted samurai, while 4 per cent (655 men) had arquebuses. This shows the great reliance the Takeda placed on their cavalry arm. A later chapter will show how these 4,254 horsemen were distributed during the charge at the Battle of Nagashino. For now it is sufficient to note that 125 of the above stayed in the siege lines, leaving 4,031 to take part in the assault on the Oda-Tokugawa lines, where there were 3,000 matchlockmen waiting for them. There were therefore three ashigaru matchlockmen on the Oda side for every four Takeda mounted samurai charging them. Under normal circumstances a cavalryman, if he survived the ashigaru's one shot, would be upon the shooter within seconds. The crucial difference at Nagashino lay in how the ashigaru were to be used.

OVERLEAF **It is dawn on the first full day of the siege of Nagashino. The castle is rising from an early morning mist that hangs along the river, and as visibility increase so the firing becomes more rapid from both sides. The view is from the south, looking across the gorge at its deepest point, the spot where Torii Sune'emon was destined to make his brave gesture. Here the siege lines are seen in close up. There are bundles of green bamboo and wooden shields from which the weary Takeda footsoldiers shoot arrows and fire guns. They are joined by three Takeda generals. Anayama Nobukimi, who is also a monk, Sanada Nobutsuna and the veteran Yamagata Masakage, whose hair is white. The details of their appearance and armour are taken from painted scrolls preserved in the Erin-ji temple near Kofu, the Takeda headquarters.**

OPPOSING PLANS

Although he was to play a decisive role in the Battle of Nagashino, Oda Nobunaga took little part and had little interest in the preliminary moves of the campaign, and was only drawn into the conflict later by the threat it posed to one of his most important allies. Oda Nobunaga then took the opportunity the situation presented to land a crushing blow on the Takeda while half their army was isolated from the security provided by their mountainous home provinces. Mikata-ga-hara had provided a similar opportunity in 1572, but at that time the Takeda army was commanded by the mighty and prudent Takeda Shingen, and the Takeda had won. Katsuyori's advance into Mikawa in 1575 was an ideal chance to settle the score.

The Nagashino campaign began on 30 May 1575 with the departure of Takeda Katsuyori from his fortified mansion of Tsutsuji-ga-saki in what is now the city of Kofu. The previous day had been the anniversary of the death of his father, Takeda Shingen, and Katsuyori had burned incense at his father's shrine. The departure for war was held with great pomp, with the raising of the three precious standards of the Takeda – the two red banners dedicated to the local *kami* (god) Suwa Myôjin and the great blue banner which bore a quotation from the writings of the Chinese military authority Sun Zi that had become the Takeda motto: 'Swift like the wind; quiet like the forest; conquer like the fire; steady as the mountain'.

Although subsequent events may indicate that the move into Mikawa province was foolhardy, this is to judge the campaign with the benefit of hindsight. The invasion of Mikawa was by no means a mere precipitate raid but a calculated attempt to take Tokugawa Ieyasu's headquarters castle of Okazaki, the capital of Mikawa. Takeda Katsuyori was simply continuing the forward aggressive policy that Shingen had set in motion with Mikata-ga-hara and Noda, and which Katsuyori had followed modestly in the intervening two years. The raid of 1575 was, however, carried out against the advice of his senior generals, who urged caution while they were still in arms against Uesugi Kenshin to the north.

The trump card that Takeda Katsuyori intended to play was a traitor in Okazaki castle, a very senior official within the Tokugawa administration known as Oga Yashiro. He handled most of the financial affairs of the provinces, and was so highly regarded that it was said that the sun could not rise without Oga Yashiro first giving it permission. In 1575, corrupted perhaps by his position, he turned traitor against the Tokugawa and offered to open the gates of Okazaki to an advance by the Takeda army. Okazaki castle was at that time commanded by Ieyasu's son Nobuyasu, while Ieyasu himself was based at Hamamatsu in Tôtômi. The loss of his home province's capital of Okazaki would lead to the speedy collapse of the Tokugawa clan.

Takeda Katsuyori therefore set out on his conquest of the Tokugawa lands, but before he reached Okazaki the plot was discovered. Oga

Ashigaru gunners in action, as depicted in a detail from a book illustration in the *Ehon Taikô-ki*. Two are firing their arquebuses from a kneeling position, while one is standing. Note how the artist has shown the smoke rising from the smouldering match in the serpentine.

守山の城を
遣かて
種村上坂を
説惑つむ

Yashiro was captured, and sentenced to the slow death of the bamboo saw, whereby the felon was buried up to his neck in the ground with his head protruding through a wooden board. Beside the board was a bamboo saw, which passers-by were invited to apply to his neck. Many availed themselves of the opportunity of executing a traitor, and Oga Yashiro died after seven days of agony. The news reached Takeda Katsuyori when he was somewhere in the vicinity of Asuke, having descended into Mikawa by one of the most convenient mountain passes. He realised that the removal of Oga from the scene meant that an attack upon Okazaki was not feasible, so he swung his army east in the direction of Tsukude. The latter was a Tokugawa possession which had bitter associations for Katsuyori because it was Tsukude that Okudaira Sadamasa had abandoned when he had returned to the Tokugawa fold.

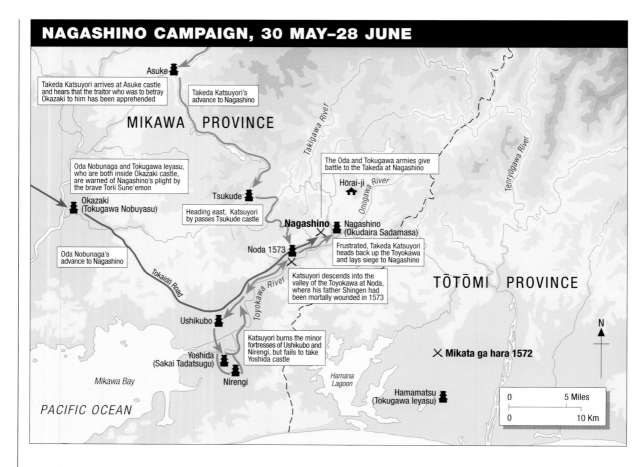

Asuke

Takeda Katsuyori arrives at Asuke castle and hears that the traitor who was to betray Okazaki to him has been apprehended

Takeda Katsuyori's advance to Nagashino

MIKAWA PROVINCE

Takigawa River

The Oda and Tokugawa armies give battle to the Takeda at Nagashino

Hōrai-ji

Onogawa River

Tenryūgawa river

Oda Nobunaga and Tokugawa Ieyasu, who are both inside Okazaki castle, are warned of Nagashino's plight by the brave Torii Sune'emon

Tsukude

Okazaki (Tokugawa Nobuyasu)

Heading east, Katsuyori by passes Tsukude castle

Nagashino

Nagashino (Okudaira Sadamasa)

Noda 1573

Frustrated, Takeda Katsuyori heads back up the Toyokawa and lays siege to Nagashino

Oda Nobunaga's advance to Nagashino

Tokaidō Road

Toyokawa River

Katsuyori descends into the valley of the Toyokawa at Noda, where his father Shingen had been mortally wounded in 1573

TŌTŌMI PROVINCE

Ushikubo

Katsuyori burns the minor fortresses of Ushikubo and Nirengi, but fails to take Yoshida castle

N

Yoshida (Sakai Tadatsugu)

Nirengi

Hamana Lagoon

✕ **Mikata ga hara 1572**

Mikawa Bay

Hamamatsu (Tokugawa Ieyasu)

PACIFIC OCEAN

0		5 Miles
0		10 Km

Tsukude was by-passed, and the Takeda continued on a cross-country route through Mikawa, determined to cause some destruction before they returned home. They joined the Toyokawa river at Noda (now Shinshiro), the scene of his father's mortal wound, and headed downstream towards the Pacific coast. On 13 June Takeda Katsuyori burned the two minor fortresses of Nirengi and Ushikubo which acted as outer defence satellites for Yoshida castle, which now lies within Toyohashi city. He then began an attack on Yoshida.

The keeper of Yoshida castle was Sakai Tadatsugu, commander of the eastern Mikawa division of the Tokugawa army and one of Ieyasu's most reliable generals. When Takeda Katsuyori arrived outside the walls he discovered to his surprise that Tokugawa Ieyasu was inside it with 5,000 men. Ieyasu had heard of Katsuyori's raid and had been following his movements for the past two weeks. Leaving his son Nobuyasu in Okazaki with 7,000 men, he had speedily reinforced the castle that he had judged correctly to be the Takeda's secondary target. It was a situation very similar to the one that had existed immediately prior to Takeda Shingen's victory at Mikata-ga-hara in 1572, with Tokugawa Ieyasu inside a castle and a large Takeda army outside it. Could Ieyasu be persuaded a second time to march his army out for a pitched battle?

The initial moves looked promising for the Takeda, as small contingents of the Tokugawa garrison sallied forth to do battle with the Takeda vanguard, who were under the command of Yamagata Masakage.

This man, then aged 60, was one of Shingen's veterans. Together with four personal retainers he engaged Mizuno Tadashige, Toda Kazuaki and Watanabe Hanzô (nicknamed 'Hanzô the Spear') and 34 others from Ieyasu's hatamoto in hand-to-hand spear fighting outside the walls. The aim of the action appears to have been little more than the achievement of samurai glory, since they were not followed by a Tokugawa army and were recalled to the castle once their combats were finished. The spear fighting was nonetheless carried out with great ferocity, helped by matchlockmen who do not appear to have respected the ancient samurai principle of single combat as an activity carried out between gentleman of equal stature. Mizuno Tadashige of the Tokugawa force had his right elbow shattered by an arquebus ball but continued to wield his spear in single combat using his left arm.

It soon became apparent that the 6,000 men now in Yoshida were not going to oblige Katsuyori with a battle outside its walls, and there was little point in beginning a siege against such a strong garrison. It would take a great deal of time and there was always the danger of enemies coming up from behind if the Takeda looked like being tied to a siege for a prolonged period. So Takeda Katsuyori decided to abandon yet another objective of the campaign, and turned his army back up the Toyokawa to the north. He had already decided to leave Noda and Tsukude alone, and being loath to leave Mikawa without some prize, he turned his attentions to the final castle along the river. This was Nagashino, held for the Tokugawa by a small garrison under one of Kaysuyori's most hated enemies: Okudaira Sadamasa. Possession of Nagashino was an asset worth having. It had passed from Tokugawa to Takeda and back again, and covered one of the mountain passes to Shinano. If Takeda Katsuyori had been frustrated in his attempts to take Okazaki and Yoshida, little Nagashino would be a good consolation prize with which to conclude his Mikawa campaign.

The site of Nagashino castle is a naturally strong rocky cliff where the rivers Takigawa and Onogawa meet to form the Toyokawa. The main section of the keep was built on the point of the triangle formed by the rivers. This photograph is taken from the modern road bridge that crosses the Toyokawa. The water level has probably fallen over the centuries, owing to water extraction.

THE SIEGE OF NAGASHINO CASTLE

The site of the castle of Nagashino is located within Hôrai town, named after the Hôrai-ji, a prominent local Buddhist temple. It lies about 24km north-east of the city of Toyohashi. The modern road follows the Toyokawa upstream, and it is at Nagashino that the vast, wide and flat rice fields begin to give way to forested mountains and the agricultural fields become terraced. The road narrows here and begins to climb beyond Nagashino into the foothills of what was the province of Shinano, the territory of the Takeda.

The castle of Nagashino dated from 1508, and had been originally constructed by Suganuma Motonari, a vassal of the Imagawa and one of the three powerful families of the eastern Mikawa area. Because of its strategic importance as the northern gateway to Mikawa province Nagashino had been captured by Takeda Shingen in 1571, and had then been returned to the Tokugawa in 1573. By 1575 it was still a Tokugawa possession, and Okudaira Sadamasa was formally appointed as keeper of Nagashino castle in early April. The castle was under his command during the siege, when he was assisted by Matsudaira Kagetada and his

A distant view of the temple of Daitsûji, the forward point of the Takeda siege lines. The road just in front of the temple building marks the approximate position of the outer defence works of the castle of Nagashino, known as the Fukube-maru. This area was the first to be lost to the Takeda assault. The hills were just as wooded during the siege.

Details of the gate and walls of Nagashino castle, as depicted on a modern copy of the famous Nagashino screen. The artist has shown a bridge crossing the Onogawa to the area of Tobigasu, but this is unsupported by historical evidence. The simple walls, plastered with clay and pierced by apertures for guns and bows, are probably accurate. The walls are topped with thatch rather than tiles.

son Matsudaira Koremasa. The garrison consisted of 500 men whose equipment included 200 matchlocks and at least one cannon.

The site of Nagashino castle is a naturally strong defensive position. It is here that the two rivers Takigawa and Onogawa join in the shape of a letter 'Y' to become the Toyokawa, and at this point their banks are cliffs of 50m high and about 50–60m apart. The castle site is therefore a triangular piece of rocky land protected on two sides by cliffs and water. From a military point of view its weakest edge was the landward side to the north and north-west, where swampy ground ran up to the forested hill of Datsûjiyama. Here the road to the north continued on into the mountains.

The castle site is very well preserved to this day, and the building of a single-track railway round its edge has served to conserve the area rather than to destroy it. Its historical importance has long been realised, and the immediate surrounding area is kept as an open field, the museum being the only building to encroach on the site.

The castle which existed in 1575 would have borne little resemblance to the graceful white buildings on stone bases which characterise surviving Japanese castles such as Himeji and Hikone. Instead its buildings were of a simple wooden construction with wooden boarded roofs. Stone was used only for the outer walls. The fortified area was small in size, being restricted by the cliffs, and the site of the preserved *hon-maru* (inner bailey) is 330m from east to west and 250m from north to south. At the time of the siege approximately one third of the area – that to the east which was on lower ground terraced out from the hill – was separated off into an enclosure called the Yagyû-guruwa. The term 'guruwa' simply means an area enclosed by earthworks. From the Yagyû-guruwa a gate, called the Yagyû-mon, afforded access down the cliff side to the river. In 1575 the whole area of the hon-maru was defended by a stone wall and a dry moat.

In addition to the hon-maru, the original castle also had a series of outer defences, the *ni no maru* (second bailey), known as the Obi-guruwa, and the *san no maru* (third bailey), called the Tomoe-guruwa. The gate from the third bailey was called the Tomoejiro-mon. All three baileys were protected on the western side by a rapidly flowing mountain stream which cascaded into the Takigawa. The stream was crossed by a bridge to an area of flatland where the defenders had established two further enclosures – an inner one protected by a wall and earthwork, called the Danjô-guruwa, and an outer one, defended only by dry moat and a partial section of wall, called the Hattori-guruwa. Here a gate called the Ote-mon led to the west. To the north the final enclosure which lay outside the san no maru and led almost to the slopes of Daitsûjiyama was called the Fukube-maru (the Fukube barbican). It stretched as far as a little stream where there was a wall and a bridge

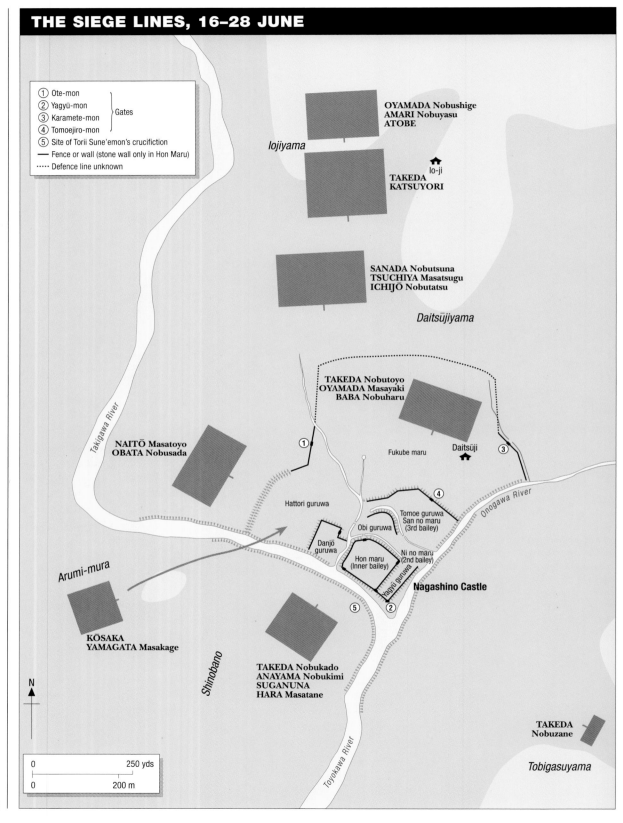

1. Ote-mon
2. Yagyū-mon ⎫
3. Karamete-mon ⎬ Gates
4. Tomoejiro-mon ⎭
5. Site of Torii Sune'emon's crucifiction
— Fence or wall (stone wall only in Hon Maru)
···· Defence line unknown

Iojiyama

OYAMADA Nobushige
AMARI Nobuyasu
ATOBE

Io-ji

TAKEDA
KATSUYORI

SANADA Nobutsuna
TSUCHIYA Masatsugu
ICHIJŌ Nobutatsu

Daitsūjiyama

Takigawa River

TAKEDA Nobutoyo
OYAMADA Masayaki
BABA Nobuharu

NAITŌ Masatoyo
OBATA Nobusada

① Ote-mon

Fukube maru

Daitsūji

③

Onogawa River

Hattori guruwa

④

Tomoe guruwa
San no maru
(3rd bailey)

Obi guruwa

Danjō
guruwa

Ni no maru
(2nd bailey)

Hon maru
(Inner bailey)

Nagashino Castle

Yagyū guruwa

Arumi-mura

⑤

②

KŌSAKA
YAMAGATA Masakage

Shinobano

TAKEDA Nobukado
ANAYAMA Nobukimi
SUGANUMA
HARA Masatane

TAKEDA
Nobuzane

Tobigasuyama

Toyokawa River

N

0   250 yds
0   200 m

leading from a gate called the Karamete-mon – which just means 'the rear gate'. The wall continued up into the trees on Daitsûjiyama , as did the wall of the Hattori-guruwa on the western side. As long as the heights of Daitsûjiyama were held by the defending army, this area covered the road to the north and added greatly to the castle's defences.

Takeda Army Dispositions

Takeda Katsuyori decided to abandon the siege of Yoshida castle on 14 June, and all his army were at Nagashino by about 16 June. In the expectation of a quick and easy victory he drew up his army in eight divisions ready for attack. Katsuyori clearly appreciated the nature of the castle's layout, and made a point of securing the hills of Daitsûjiyama and Iojiyama with a large number of troops. From there an attack could be mounted on the Fukube-maru. The hill of Iojiyama, beside which stood the temple of Io-ji, lay about 1km from the Ote-mon of the castle and in 1575 afforded an uninterrupted view of Nagashino, so this became Kaysuyori's headquarters where he stationed his personal contingent of 3,000 men. On the reverse slope of Iojiyama were Amari Nobuyasu and Oyamada Nobushige with 2,000 men as a rearguard. The vital forward area of Daitsûjiyama was covered by the veteran generals Takeda Nobutoyo, Baba Nobuharu and Oyamada Masayuki and their 3,000 troops.

To the north-west of the castle, on the flatlands beyond the Hattori-guruwa, were Ichijô Nobutatsu, Sanada Nobutsuna and Tsuchiya Masatsugu, again with 3,000 men. To the west, on the eastern bank of the Takigawa and closer to the Hattori-guruwa, were Naitô Masatoyo and Obata Nobusada with 2,500 men. The other divisions faced the castle from across the rivers. To the south of the Takigawa, in the triangular area between the Takigawa and the Toyokawa known as Shinobano, were Takeda Nobukado, Anayama Nobukimi (known better by his later Buddhist name of Anayama Baisetsu), Hara Masatane and Suganuma Sadanao with 1,500 men. To the south-west of the Takigawa, in the area called Arumi-mura, were stationed Yamagata Masakage and Kosaka Masazumi with 1,000 samurai and other ranks as a reserve corps. To the east, across the Onogawa and occupying the hill of Tobigasuyama, was the solitary division of Takeda Nobuzane with 1,000 men.

A corner tower of the castle of Hamamatsu. Nagashino castle made some limited use of stone in its defences – probably low sloping earth mounds like this one, which is faced with rough blocks. The wooden walls are also likely to have looked like this example, but without the elaborate eaves and roofing.

RIGHT **The low walls of Shôryûji castle, set upon an earth mound and topped with a wooden palisade, are typical of the mid-Sengoku period, so we may envisage parts of Nagashino castle looking like this. Shôryûji lies mid way between Kyoto and Osaka, and has recently been excavated. The outer walls have been rebuilt to enclose a public park.**

35

The Four-Day Attack

The first fighting of the siege of Nagashino occurred on 17 June, when some Takeda samurai tested the mettle of the defenders with an attack on the Ote-mon to the north-west. The following day the attack began in earnest as Takeda Katsuyori ordered an all-out assault under the cover of *taketaba* (shields made from bundles of bamboo). The defenders counter-attacked vigorously and set fire to the taketaba. According to the *Nagashino nikki* account, the bullets and arrows from within the castle caused 800 casualties among the Takeda troops. This encounter began a contest of arms that was to last with hardly a break for an exhausting four days. The garrison, although outnumbered by 30 to one, put up stiff resistance as the chronicles record. Bullet was met by bullet, and spear by spear. Early in the activity (the date is not given, but it was probably 19 June) the Takeda showed great ingenuity in their attempts to break down the defences of Nagashino castle. One potential weak point was the Yagyû-mon, the gate which led out to a cliff path down to the river on the castle side. The river was almost impossible to cross at that point, so the Takeda constructed a wooden raft and floated a detachment of soldiers down the Onogawa towards it. The defenders first greeted the sluggish craft with a hail of arrows and bullets and then with rocks, and the raft was sunk before it had a chance to be moored. It would certainly appear from this incident that the river in 1575 had much more water in it than it does today. Nowadays it would be impossible to float a raft down it at this time of year.

On 20 June the Takeda launched a night attack from two sides. The sky was cloudy, obscuring the moon, and under cover of pitch darkness the Takeda assaulted the Fukube-maru. This area measured 136m from east to west and 90m from north to south. There were no earthworks, only a wooden fence. However, it was bordered on one side by cliffs and on the other by boggy land, and it was also under the eyes of the defending garrison in the Tomoe-guruwa, who were able to cover it with gunfire. It was thus a location advantageous to hold, but would not necessarily prove a disaster if it were relinquished. Taking advantage of the darkness the Takeda troops flung hooked ropes on to the stockade walls and hauled themselves over into the Fukube-maru. Here they were met by a hail of arrows and bullets from the defenders. However, the numerical superiority of the Takeda told, and Okudaira Sadamasa ordered a withdrawal to within the Tomoe-guruwa, from which a counter-attack could be mounted. The Fukube-maru was thus effectively abandoned to the Takeda.

At the same time an attack was made against the Ote-mon, the gate to the west from the Hattori-guruwa, and Okudaira Sadamasa was forced to make the same difficult decision of withdrawing from these outer defences and pulling back into the earthworks of the castle itself. The area of the Hattori-guruwa and the Fukube-maru, which was continuous with Daitsûjiyama , had now become a 'no man's land' between the two sides. That same night the Takeda began the rapid construction of a siege tower from large diameter tree trunks. This would provide them with a platform from which they could look down into the castle itself from just outside the defences. The tower and its construction work were protected by taketaba. The work went on all night, and as dawn broke on 21 June the final rope holding it up was secured. The defenders'

ABOVE **An attack on the walls of a Sengoku castle, as shown in a detail from the *Ehon Taikô-ki* which refers to one of the forts in the area of the battle of Shizugatake. Long spears are thrust forward to break open the clay surface of the 'wattle and daub' walls. They also seem to have provided a convenient ladder for the samurai who is climbing over the tiled tops of the defences.**

response was immediate, for they had in the castle a cannon capable of firing a shot of 15–20kg. This opened up on the tower and scored a direct hit, smashing it to pieces.

The loss of the tower did not reduce the ferocity of the Takeda attack. The besiegers now controlled the former Fukube-maru and from there were able to press home attacks against the Tomoe-guruwa. This provoked a sally from within the castle, led at spear-point by Yamazaki Zenshichi, Okudaira Izumo, two samurai called Shoda and Kuroya and others. The attackers were temporarily driven off for the loss of ten casualties from within the garrison.

Early that same morning there occurred a remarkable incident described in one of the chronicles. A certain samurai called Toda Tôgorô, who was under the command of Matsudaira Matashichirô, was devoted to the worship of Hachiman, the Shinto god of war. That

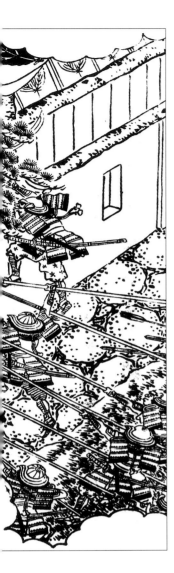

RIGHT **Samurai attack a moated castle. Nagashino probably did not possess the sophisticated stone walls shown in this picture, but it nonetheless gives a good impression of the determination of samurai to be the first into battle during a siege. Patience was not a recognisable samurai virtue.**

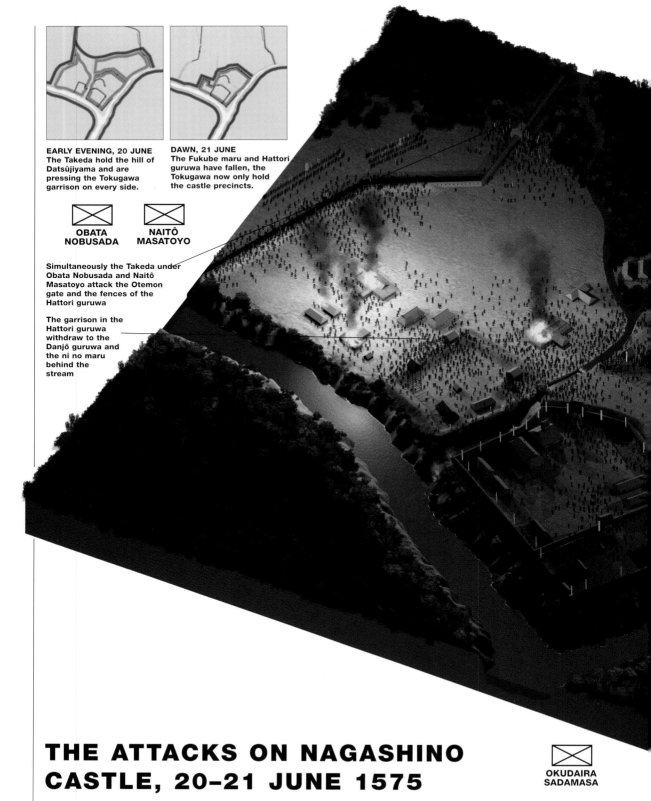

EARLY EVENING, 20 JUNE
The Takeda hold the hill of Datsûjiyama and are pressing the Tokugawa garrison on every side.

DAWN, 21 JUNE
The Fukube maru and Hattori guruwa have fallen, the Tokugawa now only hold the castle precincts.

OBATA NOBUSADA

NAITÔ MASATOYO

Simultaneously the Takeda under Obata Nobusada and Naitô Masatoyo attack the Otemon gate and the fences of the Hattori guruwa

The garrison in the Hattori guruwa withdraw to the Danjô guruwa and the ni no maru behind the stream

THE ATTACKS ON NAGASHINO CASTLE, 20–21 JUNE 1575

OKUDAIRA SADAMASA

On the nght of 20 June the Takeda forces launched an attack on the castle from two sides, these attacks carried on until the dawn of the 21st.

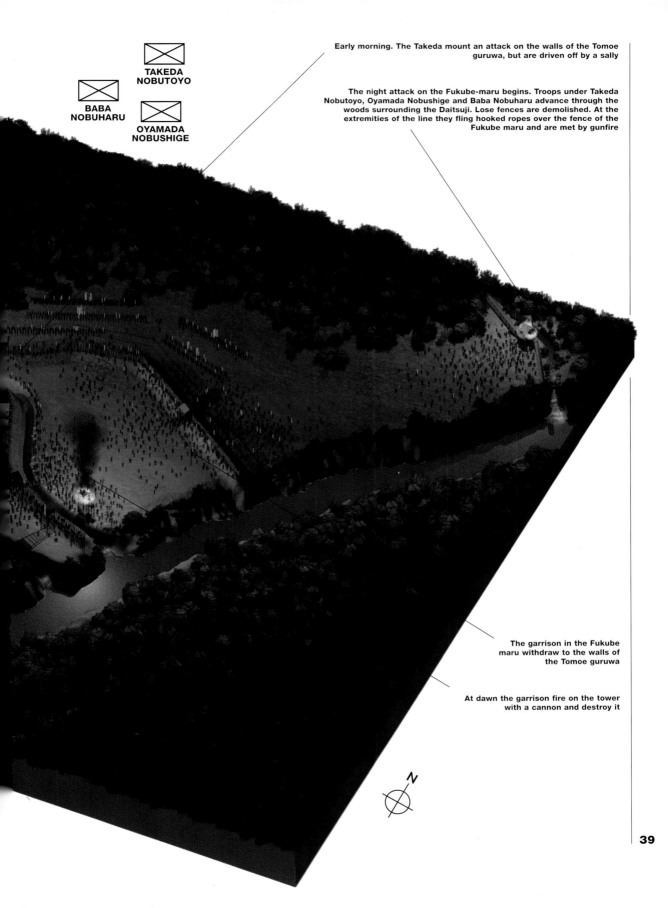

TAKEDA
NOBUTOYO

BABA
NOBUHARU

OYAMADA
NOBUSHIGE

Early morning. The Takeda mount an attack on the walls of the Tomoe guruwa, but are driven off by a sally

The night attack on the Fukube-maru begins. Troops under Takeda Nobutoyo, Oyamada Nobushige and Baba Nobuharu advance through the woods surrounding the Daitsuji. Lose fences are demolished. At the extremities of the line they fling hooked ropes over the fence of the Fukube maru and are met by gunfire

The garrison in the Fukube maru withdraw to the walls of the Tomoe guruwa

At dawn the garrison fire on the tower with a cannon and destroy it

morning he descended the path from the Yagyû-mon to the river, where he performed cold water ablutions and prayed to Hachiman for good fortune in war. He was spotted by an enemy general, who sent a samurai down to the river to despatch him, but the Takeda warrior missed his footing and fell into the water. Taking this as a sign of the god's goodwill, Tôgorô tackled the man and cut off his head, taking it back as a trophy and dedicating it, appropriately enough, to Hachiman.

This was the only good fortune Hachiman was to send that day, 21 June, because later that morning there was a new and alarming development in the garrison's fortunes. One of the strengths behind the Takeda economy was the existence of gold mines in the mountains of their provinces. Many gold miners had been drafted into the Takeda army for their tunnelling skills, and they had been hard at work since the siege began. There was a high stone wall at the western corner of the hon-maru, and on the morning of 21 June a section of it collapsed, making a considerable noise. The damage was not total, but had a considerable psychological effect on the Nagashino garrison, who had now been fighting continuously for four days and nights. The Takeda had rotated their troops, a luxury which the 500-strong garrison could not afford. Instead, between attacks they had needed to work at strengthening or shoring up their defences by excavating a dry moat around the hon-maru and using the soil for another earthwork wall.

As expected, a furious attack followed the mining, and 21 June saw the fiercest and most intense fighting of the siege. By evening the defenders had lost to the Takeda both the third bailey and the

The area of the former castle of Nagashino is well shown in this distant view. The houses of the town of Horai fill the area that was formerly the second and third bailey, the Obi-guruwa and the Tomoe-guruwa. The railway bridge crosses the Takigawa along the edge of the *hon-maru* (inner bailey), which is remarkably well preserved.

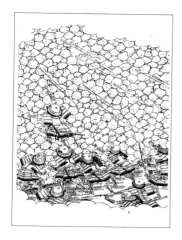

Climbing a castle wall. This dramatic detail from the *Ehon Taikô-ki* shows the indomitable samurai spirit at its best, as the warriors clamber up the rough stone wall like so many black beetles, oblivious of the hail of arrows pouring down on top of them.

OVERLEAF **Torii Sune'emon has daringly escaped from the castle, swimming the river and walking to Okazaki to tell them that relief is urgently needed. With his generals and allies beside him, Oda Nobunaga receives him in the audience hall. His suit of armour is on a stand in the corner. The room is lit by oil lamps on stands. Torii is still somewhat dishevelled, in contrast to the senior samurai who sit in full regalia, wearing jinbaori with their helmets beside them. The urgency of his mission is illustrated by the remarkable fact that he has been allowed in without removing his sandals. Nobunaga's suit of armour is one that he is known to have worn.**

Danjô-guruwa, the earthwork that had been the only extension of the castle left projecting across the stream on the western side. All that was left of Nagashino castle was now the area covered by the hon-maru, the Yagyu-guruwa and ni no maru. Most importantly, the Takeda had succeeded in destroying the castle's storehouses.

By this time both sides were growing tired. Having failed with towers, mines and rafts after five days of fighting, Takeda Katsuyori was beginning to realise that the castle was not going to fall to an assault. The Takeda had also suffered an unexpectedly high proportion of casualties, but as the provisions store of the castle was now gone, Katsuyori estimated that the defenders only had a few days supplies left. He therefore decided to starve the garrison out. The attack was suspended, and while sniper fire and the occasional bombardment continued, a strong fence was begun which would totally surround the castle. It ran along the approximate line of the former outer defence works. For good measure, ropes were strung across the three rivers, with nets hanging down into the water, 'so that even an ant could not get out'. Clappers were attached to the ropes to provide warning of anyone entering or leaving by that route.

The blockade began on 22 June and the garrison began to adjust to these new conditions of warfare. A 22-year old *samurai-taishô* (commander of a samurai unit) called Imaizumi Naiki stuck his head out of an arrow port to judge the progress of the siege and was seriously wounded by a sniper. He later died. In another sniper incident a certain Gotô Sukeza'emon was hit by a bullet, collapsed into a coma and never regained consciousness. Apart from these casualties, a sad loss to the garrison was the death from illness of the veteran warrior Shidara Shigetsugu, aged 79. He had served Tokugawa Ieyasu's father, and his experience of warfare had proved invaluable.

All that the Takeda now needed was time. Six years later, at Tottori castle, a garrison would be almost reduced to cannibalism before their siege was over. Should no relieving force arrive, and none was apparently on the way, Nagashino castle would probably suffer the same fate within a week.

The Exploit of Torii Sune'emon

At this point in the siege there occurred one of the most celebrated incidents of samurai heroism in Japanese history. Torii Sune'emon was a 34-year-old samurai of Mikawa province and a retainer of Okudaira Sadamasa. His bravery was renowned and he was also very familiar with the territory, so he volunteered for the suicidal task of escaping from the castle and making his way to Okazaki to request help from Tokugawa Ieyasu.

A request had in fact already been sent before the blockade began, but no reply had been received, so the defenders were unaware that both Tokugawa Ieyasu and Oda Nobunaga had decided that the siege of Nagashino was a matter to be taken seriously and were planning to march to its relief. Oda Nobunaga had left Gifu on 20 June, travelled via Atsuta and arrived at Okazaki to join Ieyasu the following day. There was undoubtedly an element of self-interest in Nobunaga's decision to throw the whole weight of his army behind an attempt to relieve a fortress of an ally when his own territories were not immediately threatened. However, Nobunaga was shrewd enough to realise that if he did not

support the Tokugawa they might be swayed towards an alliance with the Takeda against him. So the force was committed unconditionally, and the outcome also promised a showdown with Takeda Katsuyori, which was itself a welcome opportunity. Yet clearly neither appreciated the extreme urgency of the situation, which made Torii Sune'emon's mission all the more important.

At midnight on 23 June Torii Sune'emon left the castle through the Yagyû-mon, climbed down the cliff path and slipped into the river. He swam down the Toyokawa until he reached the nets which the Takeda had strung across it. He cut a hole in the net under the water without making a

sound, swam through and continued on his way. At dawn on 24 June he lit a beacon on Mount Gambo as a pre-arranged signal to inform the garrison that he had managed to get through. Then he carried on to Okazaki where he was warmly welcomed and admired for his feat. Torii Sune'emon reported that the castle had by then only about three days supply of food left, and that when that had gone all that Okudaira Sadamasa could do was to offer to commit *hara-kiri* to save the lives of his men. The castle would inevitably fall. Oda and Tokugawa promised to move the next day.

ABOVE **Torii Sune'emon swims under water. This modern painting in the Nagashino Castle Preservation Hall shows Torii Sune'emon cutting through the nets in the river with his dagger. From here he proceeded to Okazaki castle with the news that the garrison were near to collapse.**

An old print (damaged by damp) showing Torii being forced to shout to the defenders of Nagashino across the Takigawa. There is considerable artistic licence in this picture. The castle of Nagashino, in reality no more than a large stockade reinforced with stone, has become a mighty fortress like Osaka castle, with a huge moat.

Torii Sune'emon then began the hazardous journey back to the castle to let Okudaira know that help was on its way and that he only needed to hold out for just that little bit longer. Again, as pre-arranged, Torii Sune'emon lit three beacons to inform the garrison of the good news, but instead of waiting for the relieving force to come along behind him, Torii Sune'emon attempted to re-enter the castle by the way he had departed. Unfortunately the Takeda had seen the beacons and concluded that someone from the castle had escaped, so this time they were ready for him. They spread sand on the river bank to disclose footprints and rigged up bells on ropes across the river where there had been none before. Torii Sune'emon was caught and brought before Takeda Katsuyori.

Throughout Japanese history examples of samurai bravery have been celebrated by friend and foe alike, and Torii Sune'emon's exploit was no exception. Katsuyori listened to his story, including the intelligence that a relieving force was on its way, and offered the captive Torii Sune'emon service in the Takeda army. Torii Sune'emon apparently agreed, but the suspicious Katsuyori insisted that he demonstrate this change of allegiance by addressing the garrison and telling them that no army was on its way and that surrender was the only course of action. The spot chosen for Torii Sune'emon's address was the place where the two lines were at their closest – the riverbank of the Takigawa at Shinobano. Some accounts say he was tied to a cross, others that he merely stood on the cliff edge to bellow out his message, but it was by crucifixion that he met his end. Instead of urging the defenders to surrender, he shouted to them to stand fast as help was indeed on its way. One account speaks of spears being thrust into his body as he uttered these words, others of his execution later.

LEFT **Torii Sune'emon is caught by the ropes. Suspecting that someone had escaped from the beleagured castle the Takeda stretched ropes across the river with bells attached to them. Their ringing gave Torii Sune'emon away to the watching sentries, and he was captured.**

However or whenever he died, the example of Torii Sune'emon is one of the classic stories of samurai heroism. Many in the Takeda army were moved by his example. One retainer of the Takeda, Ochiai

Michihisa, was so impressed that he had a flag painted with an image of Torii Sune'emon tied to the cross, his body covered in blood. When Takeda Katsuyori was finally defeated in 1582 Ochiai became a retainer of Tokugawa Ieyasu, and the flag, which he used as his personal banner, still exists.

Whatever the effect Torii Sune'emon's bravery had on the enemy, its effect on the garrison was inspiring. A relieving force was on its way and they only had to hold out for perhaps two more days.

LEFT **A detail from the damaged print shows one of the Takeda commanders, Anayama Baisetsu Nobukimi, ordering the control of Torii Sune'emon. Anayama is identified by the mon on his blue banner. He is attended by two footsoldiers who wear unusual jingasa with very pronounced conical shapes.**

ABOVE **Torii Sune'emon is brought to the bank of the Takigawa in this lively modern interpretation on display in the Preservation Hall of Nagashino Castle. On the whole the details are fairly good, but again the castle is made impossibly ornate and large, and includes a drawbridge. The artist also does not seem to know what an ashigaru's jingasa actually looked like.**

BELOW, RIGHT **One retainer of the Takeda, a certain Ochiai Michihisa, was so impressed by Torii Sune'emon's bravery that he had a banner painted depicting the hero of Nagashino. This copy of the banner depicting Torii is being flown in the courtyard of the Nagashino castle site in preparation for the annual festival in May.**

THE BATTLE OF NAGASHINO

The Takeda Siege Lines: 27 June, Evening

Now that he knew a relieving force was on its way Takeda Katsuyori held council with his senior officers, and received considerable differences of opinion over what to do. Shingen's veterans, such as Baba Nobuharu, Naitô Masatoyo, Yamagata Masakage and Oyamada Nobushige, were for making an honourable withdrawal to Kai province. The younger ones were for fighting. Men like Atobe Katsusuke scorned the advice of their elders and called it a disgrace that the ever-victorious Takeda army should even consider withdrawing.

Katsuyori was inclined to agree with the younger ones. He no doubt thought that his honour was at stake. He had left Tsutsuji-ga-saki under the great blue banner with half the Takeda army and had first been forced to cancel the attack on Okazaki and then abandon the attack on Yoshida. Now he had failed to reduce a garrison that was outnumbered by 30 to one. The campaign had lasted nearly a month, and all Katsuyori had achieved was the burning of two minor satellite fortresses. To a

Starvation during the siege of Tottori. The most horrific siege in samurai history was the one conducted by Toyotomi Hideyoshi against the castle of Tottori in 1581. The defenders were eventually reduced to cannibalism in order to survive. This was the fate that Takeda Katsuyori had in store for the defenders of Nagashino. Note the detail of the interior of a castle's walls.

The confluence of the rivers Takigawa and Onogawa as seen from the water level. Above soars the cliff on which Nagashino castle was built. To the right lies the site of the Yagyû-mon, the water-gate, out of which Torii Sune'emon escaped to bring help. The river was much higher during the siege, as we know that the attackers were able to float a raft down it. This would be impossible nowadays.

OVERLEAF In this plate the allied Oda/Tokugawa army take a brief rest on their way to the relief of Nagashino. On the left we see one of Tokugawa Ieyasu's elite mounted messengers (identifiable by the character 'go' on his sashimono) who is engaged in conversation with Sakakibara Yasumasa. Yasumasa has seated himself on a tree stump and, even in this relaxed and comparatively safe position, a personal attendant stands immediately behind him, while an ashigaru bodyguard flanks him with a spear. Shielding his eyes from the sun is Sakai Tadatsugu, another Tokugawa retainer, whose sashimono flag bears a depiction of a death's head. Behind them the Tokugawa army marches on. We see the great golden standard, and the flag presented to Tokugawa Ieyasu by the Jodo monks of Okazaki, and many nobori banners bearing Tokugawa mon. The red suns on white are Sakai troops. Details of the two general's suits of armour are taken from actual examples preserved in Japan which they are believed to have worn at about this time. Sakai's death's head flag is on display in the new museum devoted to the battle of Nagashino in Shinshiro, immediately adjacent to the battlefield.

samurai general, particularly one living under the shadow of a great father, the failure of the 1575 Mikawa raid would be an unbearable disgrace. The fact that his most senior officers were advocating such a course of action may well have served to make the potential loss of face that much keener for Katsuyori. To add to the failure of the siege by running from the two armies whom his father had defeated only three years earlier would have turned the knife further in the wound. To Katsuyori, obsessed to the point of irrationality by samurai honour and a need to emulate his father, even defeat by Oda Nobunaga might be preferable to running away from him. For the second time in the campaign the memory of Mikata-ga-hara played a crucial role in a military decision. Why should he, Katsuyori, not emulate Shingen by defeating the same enemies in battle?

There were several very good reasons why that was unlikely to happen. For the Takeda the situation at Nagashino was Mikata-ga-hara in reverse. At Mikata-ga-hara Takeda Shingen had enticed a Tokugawa army of 11,000 out of Hamamatsu castle to attack his massive 25,000-man force. The events of the previous week had shown that Tokugawa Ieyasu had learned his lesson and was not to be enticed out of Yoshida. Instead, Oda Nobunaga with his 38,000 now seemed to be enticing the Takeda with their 15,000 from their secure siege lines. It was an uncomfortable parallel for the veterans of 1572, but soon even the old generals had to accept that Katsuyori was determined to meet Nobunaga in battle, and their techniques of persuasion changed from urging a tactical withdrawal to meeting Oda Nobunaga on ground of their own choosing.

Baba Nobuharu suggested that if there was to be a fight it should be conducted from within Nagashino castle. The Takeda should therefore make a determined effort to take the fortress before the allied army arrived. He reasoned that since the matchlockmen would only be able to get in two shots apiece before the Takeda samurai reached the walls, no more than a thousand casualties could be expected before a hand-to-hand fight started, and in this the Takeda would certainly prove victorious through sheer weight of numbers. They could then face the

The night before the battle Takeda Katsuyori held a council of war with his generals, at which the fateful decision was made to attack the relieving force brought to Nagashino by Oda Nobunaga. This painted scroll in the Nagashino Castle Preservation Hall depicts that historic moment. Katsuyori sits at the top left, while his generals express emotion at their coming doom.

Oda and Tokugawa from within the walls, with the Takigawa acting as a forward moat.

However, this view did not prevail. It was Katsuyori's final decision that the Takeda would meet the relieving army in a pitched battle the following morning. The old generals had followed Shingen loyally and had transferred that loyalty to his son. Unlike Katsuyori, they realised that to fight Nobunaga with such a disadvantage of numbers and ground was almost suicidal, but their duty now meant that they must die with him. Four of the old Twenty-Four Generals – Baba Nobuharu, Naitô Masatoyo, Yamagata Masakage and Tsuchiya Masatsugu – exchanged a symbolic farewell cup of water together and prepared to take on the tremendous odds.

The Arrival of the Oda-Tokugawa Army: 27 June, Evening

As they had promised to Torii Sune'emon, Oda Nobunaga and Tokugawa Ieyasu left Okazaki castle at the head of a force of some 38,000 men on 25 June. The day after their departure the Oda-Tokugawa army reached Noda castle, and left again early the following morning, 27 June. Towards evening they were five or six km west of Nagashino on the plain of Shidarahara. Here Oda Nobunaga selected his positions. It was sufficiently far from the castle to enable him to arrange his forces without immediate interruption. According to contemporary descriptions, Oda Nobunaga dressed in style, wearing a fine yoroi armour. One of his attendants carried his helmet, an elaborate affair rather like a sombrero in shape. Other servants carried his weapons and three white banners on which were designs of a Japanese coin. To the rear was kept the packhorse supply unit, while the fighting men were arranged in a formation that made best use of the ground and took into account the Takeda's prowess with cavalry.

The initial positions adopted on arrival allowed Nobunaga to secure the nearby hills, with the left flank protected by forested mountains and the right by the Toyokawa. Oda Nobunaga's headquarters were set on Gokurakujiyama, to the rear. To the north, on Nobunaga's left, was Kitabatake Nobuo on Midoyama. Forward of him, on Tenjinyama, was Oda Nobutada. Further contingents of the Oda army moved forward to

occupy other hills. Sakuma Nobumori, Ikeda Nobuteru, Niwa Nagahide and Takigawa Kazumasu based themselves on Chayasuriyama, and the others clustered around it. Two Tokugawa contingents – Tokugawa Nobuyasu and Ishikawa Kazumasa, commander of the western Mikawa force – held Matsuoyama, slightly in advance of the Oda main body. The rest of the Tokugawa force spread out along the next set of hills, closer to the Takeda siege lines. Tokugawa Ieyasu made his overnight base on Danjôyama, along with Okubo Tadayo, Honda Tadakatsu, Sakakibara Yasumasa, Hiraiwa Chikayoshi, Sakai Tadatsugu, Torii Mototada, Naito Ienaga and the others. The Tokugawa army totalled 8,000 men.

It is quite clear that the Oda-Tokugawa dispositions were almost totally controlled by fear of the Takeda cavalry. Both the allied commanders had suffered its effects at Mikata-ga-hara, so once again the experience of that battle was to play a vital part. One effect was the selection of ground. The Oda-Tokugawa positions looked across the plain of Shidarahara towards the castle, which could not be seen because of further hills in the way, but it was no flat plain like Mikata-ga-hara. About 100m in front of them flowed the little Rengogawa, which acted as a forward defence for the positions Oda Nobunaga had chosen.

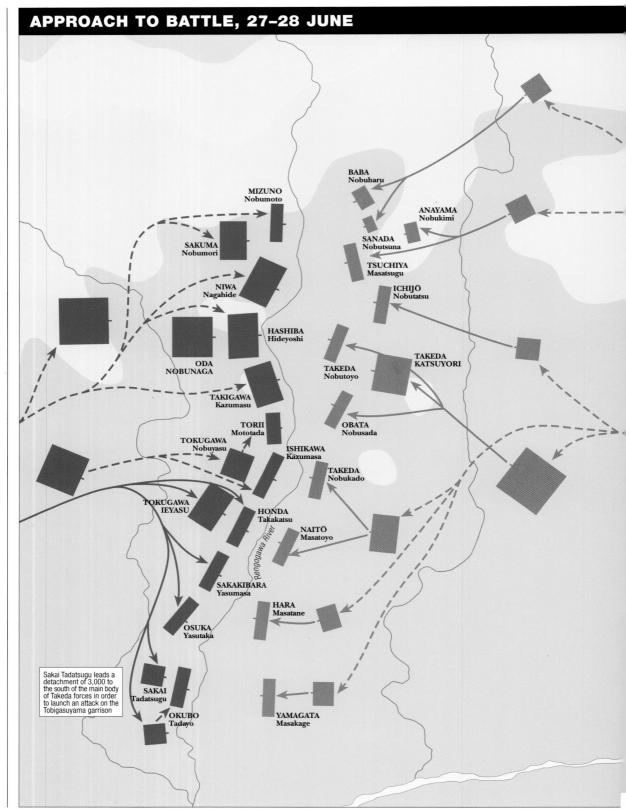

MIZUNO
Nobumoto

BABA
Nobuharu

ANAYAMA
Nobukimi

SAKUMA
Nobumori

SANADA
Nobutsuna

TSUCHIYA
Masatsugu

NIWA
Nagahide

ICHIJŌ
Nobutatsu

HASHIBA
Hideyoshi

ODA
NOBUNAGA

TAKEDA
Nobutoyo

TAKEDA
KATSUYORI

TAKIGAWA
Kazumasu

TORII
Mototada

OBATA
Nobusada

TOKUGAWA
Nobuyasu

ISHIKAWA
Kazumasa

TAKEDA
Nobukado

TOKUGAWA
IEYASU

HONDA
Takakatsu

NAITŌ
Masatoyo

Rengogawa River

SAKAKIBARA
Yasumasa

HARA
Masatane

OSUKA
Yasutaka

Sakai Tadatsugu leads a
detachment of 3,000 to
the south of the main body
of Takeda forces in order
to launch an attack on the
Tobigasuyama garrison

SAKAI
Tadatsugu

OKUBO
Tadayo

YAMAGATA
Masakage

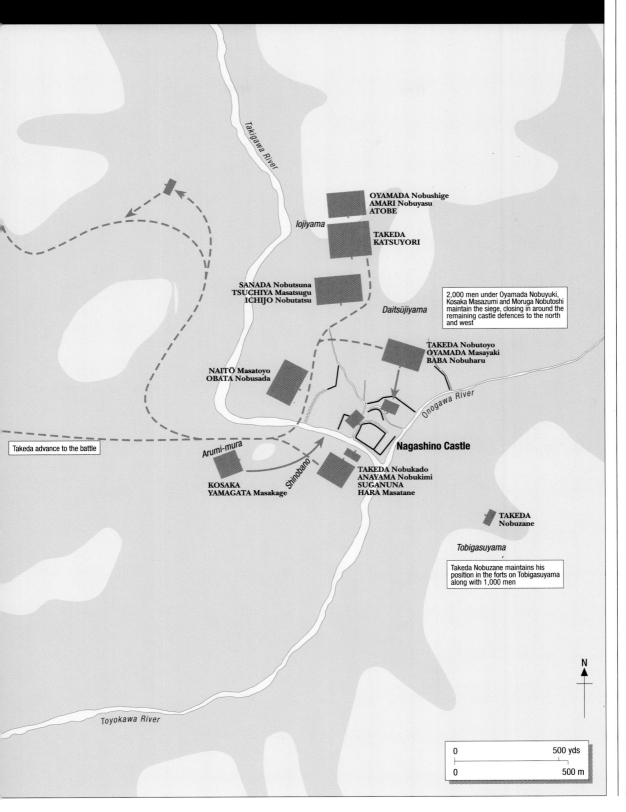

OYAMADA Nobushige
AMARI Nobuyasu
ATOBE

TAKEDA
KATSUYORI

Iojiyama

SANADA Nobutsuna
TSUCHIYA Masatsugu
ICHIJO Nobutatsu

Daitsūjiyama

2,000 men under Oyamada Nobuyuki,
Kosaka Masazumi and Moruga Nobutoshi
maintain the siege, closing in around the
remaining castle defences to the north
and west

TAKEDA Nobutoyo
OYAMADA Masayaki
BABA Nobuharu

NAITŌ Masatoyo
OBATA Nobusada

Onogawa River

Takeda advance to the battle

Arumi-mura

Shinobano

Nagashino Castle

KOSAKA
YAMAGATA Masakage

TAKEDA Nobukado
ANAYAMA Nobukimi
SUGANUNA
HARA Masatane

TAKEDA
Nobuzane

Tobigasuyama

Takeda Nobuzane maintains his
position in the forts on Tobigasuyama
along with 1,000 men

Takigawa River

Toyokawa River

N

| 0 | 500 yds |
| 0 | 500 m |

Although sluggish and shallow, it had some steep banks, which would slow down the horsemen.

Oda Nobunaga also clearly appreciated the need to give his matchlockmen some form of physical protection, so the Oda army had brought with it a large quantity of cut timber with which to build a palisade. Half way between the forested edge of the hill and the river Oda Nobunaga's troops erected this loose triple fence of stakes, stretching from the point where today the Rengogawa is crossed by a bridge to the north, where Ikeda Nobuteru was positioned. It was not a continuous construction, but was staggered over three alternate layers, with many gaps to allow for counter-attack. It also stopped short of the Toyokawa, because here, on the right flank, there was not the same cover to the rear that the hills provided for the rest of its length. The forests of the left flank provided some protection from encirclement, and Nobunaga must have decided to risk his right wing rather than weakening the whole line by spreading his defences too thinly.

Behind the fence the matchlockmen would be stationed, giving them a good range over the Rengogawa and the attacking cavalry. The total front of the Oda-Tokugawa army stretched for about 2,100m.

The Opposing Lines: 27 June, Night

That night Takeda Katsuyori made the final decision to give battle to the relieving force. Plans were drawn up for who should lead the attack and who should remain at Nagashino to continue the siege. The battle arrangement was to be four divisions – right, centre and left, with a headquarters unit to the rear. The four divisions would total 12,000 men leaving 3,000 to continue the siege. Of these, 2,000 under Oyamada Nobuyuki, Kôsaka Masazumi and Muroga Nobutoshi closed in on the

The hill of Tobigasu, looking up from the site of Nagashino castle across the Onogawa. This was the location of the dawn raid by Sakai Tadatsugu against the camp of Takeda Nobuzane. The terraced fields still follow the outlines of the field fortifications prepared by the Takeda for the siege of Nagashino.

OVERLEAF The defence line of the Oda/Tokugawa army was not protected by a continuous fence, but one that was staggered to allow a counter attack. Here one of the gaps has provided a natural lure for one detachment of Takeda cavalry under the command of Obata Masamori (also called Nobusada). The famous volleys of gunfire have done their worst, but several hours of fierce hand to hand fighting are still in prospect, and a particularly fierce encounter is about to begin. Taking advantage of a brief lull in the gunfire Obata's troops charge full tilt at the gap in the fence. Defending the line are the troops of Torii Mototada, one of the finest of the Tokugawa samurai. As the gunners pull back to regroup the footsoldiers with their long spears come into their own.

The northern slope of Tobigasu, looking down towards the castle.

west and north sides of the remaining castle defences. Across the Onogawa, Takeda Nobuzane kept up his lonely vigil from the hill of Tobigasu with the remaining 1,000 men.

While Katsuyori deliberated, a similar council of war was taking place in the Oda headquarters. As Oda Nobunaga sat with his generals he was approached by Sakai Tadatsugu of the Tokugawa force, who suggested launching a surprise attack against the Takeda siege lines as the Takeda army advanced. Sakai Tadatsugu had successfully carried out a similar manoeuvre at Mikata-ga-hara in 1572. Nobunaga did not appear to be at all enthusiastic about the plan, and upbraided Sakai Tadatsugu for his presumption in speaking out of turn, the latter retired somewhat hurt. However, Nobunaga interviewed him in private later, and assured him that he supported his plan. His anger had merely been a camouflage to throw any spies off the scent. To launch a rear attack simultaneously, with the Takeda advance away from the security of their siege lines, would be a tremendous psychological advantage. As proof of his support Nobunaga gave Sakai Tadatsugu a detachment of 500 matchlockmen under the command of Kanamori Nagachika of the elite aka horô-shû. This gesture clearly shows how confident Nobunaga was of stopping the Takeda cavalry the following day.

The raiding party was 3,000 strong. Sakai Tadatsugu was in overall command, assisted by Matsudaira Ietada, Matsudaira Tadatsugu, Honda Hirotaka, Honda Yasushige, Makino Narimune, Okudaira Tadayoshi, Suganuma Sadamitsu, Nishikyô Iekazu, Shidara Sadamichi and Abe

In this fine print, which is one of Yoshitoshi's famous series 'One hundred aspects of the moon' Sakai Tadatsugu leads the raid on Tobigasu which coincided with the battle of Nagashino. Yoshitoshi has given Sakai Tadatsugu a sashimono in the form of a three-dimensional death's head, made of wood.

Tadamasa, while Okudaira Nobumitsu and Endô Hidemochi acted as guides.

The Sakai force left at midnight under the cover of a heavy rainstorm. Being guided by local men who were familiar with the territory even in darkness, the army covered the 8km safely. They swung widely to the south, bypassing the Takeda lines and approaching the Tobigasuyama forts from the rear. There they waited patiently for the morning.

Oda/Tokugawa Lines at Shidarahara: 28 June, 05.00

As dawn broke over Shidarahara, Oda Nobunaga made his final dispositions. Retaining his command post to the rear on Gokurakujiyama, he placed his eldest son, Nobutada, in charge of the rearguard and moved himself up to the prepared positions behind the fence. The palisade had been completed overnight, and in the morning it was inspected by Ishikawa Kazumasa and Torii Mototada to ensure that it would not allow an enemy horse to jump over it.

Behind the 2,000m palisade Nobunaga placed his remaining 3,000

RIGHT **An aerial view of the immediate area of Nagashino castle. The 'Y' shape of the river is clearly shown. Torii Sune'emon was crucified next to the location of the present railway bridge. The attack on Tobigasu took place from the wooded hills in the bottom right hand corner on to the forest to the north of the hill.**

matchlockmen. The gunners, arranged three ranks deep, were under the command of members of Nobunaga's horô-shû, his finest samurai. Their normal duties were to act as his personal bodyguard, and for Nobunaga to use them to command lower class missile troops shows the immense importance Nobunaga attached to the role of the ashigaru gunners. It also shows that Nobunaga appreciated that firm discipline would be crucial. His plan was for the matchlockmen to fire rotating volleys as the Takeda cavalry approached, and for this to succeed the seven men of the horô-shû would have to exercise complete control. The matchlockmen had kept their weapons and their fuses dry during the rain – a lesson Nobunaga had learned the hard way from the Ikkô-ikki at Nagashima in 1573.

The Oda-Tokugawa line now stood as follows. On the extreme right wing, where clumps of trees led down to the Toyokawa, was Okubo Tadayo. He was 44 years old and had served in all Ieyasu's campaigns. His black and white standard had been seen next to Ieyasu's own at the battle

ABOVE **Shibata Katsuie, one of Nobunaga's generals, as seen in his statue in Fukui.**

61

龍ヶ鼻の本陣の
安長十一郎左
衛門進藤の繖を
視く歎息す

Oda Nobunaga sits in camp. In this page from the *Ehon Taikô-ki* Oda Nobunaga is shown with his mon on the breastplate of his armour. The insignia of several of his generals appear on the flags, including the butterfly of Ikeda and the crosses of Niwa.

of the Anegawa. His was the only position at Nagashino not covered by the fence. To some extent he was protected by trees, but the ground was flat, and his 1,000-strong contingent had been given a 'roving commission' to deal with any attempted encircling movement. Here he would receive the charge of one of the Takeda's finest cavalry commanders, Yamagata Masakage.

Next to Okubo, and protected by the end of the fence, was Osuka Yasutaka and Sakakibara Yasumasa, aged 27 and another faithful Tokugawa fudai. Each commanded 1,000 men. Along with Sakai Tadatsugu, Honda Tadakatsu and Ii Naomasa (who was not present at Nagashino) he was reckoned to be one of Ieyasu's *shitennô* – his four most loyal followers. Honda Tadakatsu was next along the line with a further 1,000 troops, and was instantly recognisable by the antlers on his helmet. He had the honour of having Tokugawa Ieyasu immediately behind him in the battle with his 2,000 men. Here flew the golden fan standard of the Tokugawa, and 20 white banners bearing the Tokugawa mon (badge). Almost in the centre of the line were Ishikawa Kazumasa with 1,000 and Torii Mototada with 800, both trusted retainers of the Tokugawa. Ieyasu's son Tokugawa Nobuyasu, then aged 16 and getting his first taste of battle, formed the second rank behind them, with 1,000 men. They were to face the charge from Takeda Katsuyori's centre corps, under Naitô Masatoyo.

Next to Torii stood the first of Nobunaga's contingents in the person of Takigawa Kazumasu. Next to him was Nobunaga's greatest general of all: Hashiba Hideyoshi, later to be known as Toyotomi Hideyoshi, the 'Napoleon of Japan'. As guard unit he had the honour of having Oda

Nobunaga's personal contingent immediately behind him. Niwa Nagahide was next along, and the line was concluded behind the fence by Mizuno Nobumoto, supported to the rear by Sakuma Nobumori.

The Takeda Advance: 28 June, 05.00

As noted above, each of the four Takeda divisions consisted of about 3,000 men. Using the figures from the *Kôyô Gunkan*, it is possible to be quite precise about the composition of the four contingents. In the tables which follow, the number of mounted troops is given, to which are added a small number for the named individuals (there were more than one present from certain families) and their attendants at two each. The analysis reveals that the forward three divisions were almost completely cavalry units, the only foot present being the personal attendants of the horsemen.

The right wing was under the overall command of Anayama Nobukimi. He was one of Shingen's veterans and a member of the goshinrui-shû. As a result, his samurai and ashigaru wore the Takeda mon on their flags, while his personal banner retained its own mon. Baba Nobuharu led the vanguard with 120 mounted samurai. He was a fudai and one of the Takeda's most experienced field commanders. The brothers Sanada Nobutsuna and Sanada Masateru followed. They were of the *sakikatashû*, the families taken on by the Takeda after conquest. The Sanada family, from Shinano province, had long proved their loyalty and worth to the Takeda. Tsuchiya Masatsugu and Ichijô Nobutatsu completed the right wing. The former had fought at Mikata-ga-hara with great distinction. The latter was in the goshinrui-shû and was a cousin of Takeda Katsuyori. He commanded 200 horsemen. The right wing was

In this section from a painted screen depicting the battle of the Anegawa in 1570 we see two prominent characters who fought on the Oda side at Nagashino five years later. Tokugawa Ieyasu sits in command beside the two flags proclaiming the motto of the Jôdo sect of Buddhism – 'Renounce this polluted world and attain the Pure Land'. The black flag indicates the presence of Okubo Tadayo, who commanded the vulnerable right wing at Nagashino, where there was no fence for protection. His troops met the onslaught of the veteran general Yamagata Masakage.

directed against the extreme left wing of the Oda army, under Hashiba and Sakuma.

RIGHT WING

Anayama Nobukimi (commander)	200
Baba Nobuharu (vanguard)	120
Sanada Nobutsuna and Sanada Masateru	250
Tsuchiya Masatsugu	100
Ichijô Nobutatsu	200
Tokita Tosho	10
Imogawa Ennosuke	60
Unnamed samurai from the Shinano sakikata-shû	60
Other named individuals	12
Unmounted attendants to the above	2,024
Total	**3,036**

The centre companies were to be about 3,000 men under the overall command of Takeda Nobukado, Katsuyori's uncle, whose men, including 80 horsemen, wore a white Takeda mon on black flags. He attacked the section of fence defended by Ishikawa Kazumasa. The vanguard was led by Naitô Masatoyo, who charged home against Honda Tadakatsu. They were supported by the veteran fudai Hara Masatane, who was particularly prized for his feel for ground in strategic planning. The western Kôzuke sakikata-shû supplied Wada Narimori, Annaka Kageshige and Gomi Takashige plus unnamed units of 14 horsemen. Within the centre company was the largest single contingent of horsemen in the Takeda army. This was a 500-strong unit under Obata Nobusada, also of the western Kôzuke sakikata-shû.

CENTRE COMPANY

Takeda Nobukado (commander)	80
Naitô Masatoyo (vanguard)	250
Hara Masatane	120
Obata Nobusada	500
Annaka Kageshige	150
Wada Narimori	30
Western Kôzuke (unnamed)	14
Other named individuals	9
Unmounted attendants to the above	2306
Total	**3459**

The left wing was a further 3,000 men under the overall command of Takeda Nobutoyo, a cousin of Katsuyori. He was the son of the great Takeda Nobushige, who had been killed at Kawanakajima in 1561. He rode under his late father's personal banner of a white disc on black. The vanguard of the left wing was in the most experienced hands of all. Yamagata Masakage was 60 years old and, following the example of his late brother, dressed all his troops, 300 of whom were mounted, in red armour. His flag was a white flower on black. The balance of the 3,000 included the names of individual samurai, with varying numbers of followers. Among them were Ogasawara Nobumine, Matsuoka Ukyô (Shinano sakikata-shû), Suganuma Sadanao (Mikawa/Tôtômi sakikata-shû), the veteran Oyamada Nobushige, the young Atobe Katsusuke and the fudai Amari Nobuyasu.

LEFT WING	
Takeda Nobutoyo (commander)	200
Yamagata Masakage (vanguard)	300
Nagasaka Jûza'emon	40
Atobe Katsusuke	300
Amari Nobuyasu	100
Oyamada Nobushige	200
Suganuma Sadanao	40
Matsuoka Ukyô	50
Other named individuals	12
Attendants to the above	2,484
Total	**3,726**

The centre company to the rear, which was Takeda Katsuyori's headquarters unit, set up a base within a *maku* (field curtain) on the hill overlooking Shidarahara. From here Takeda Katsuyori could control the operation and would be in a position to join in the fighting later if necessary. The unit was composed of a number of Takeda Katsuyori's closest and youngest relatives on the field, drawn from the goshinrui-shû as samurai hatamoto. They were led by Takeda Katsuyori himself, along with Takeda Nobutomo – Katsuyori's cousin, Takeda Nobumitsu – a son of the late Shingen, aged 22 and therefore Katsuyori's uncle, and Mochizuki Nobumasa – another cousin in the shinrui-shû who was the younger brother of Takeda Nobutoyo, aged 25. The balance of the division was made up from the hatamoto ashigaru. This contingent was again 3,000 strong, and was to advance to the attack through the Kiyoida area, directly across from the castle to the fence. They eventually went into the charge opposite Oda Nobunaga's headquarters unit.

TAKEDA HEADQUARTERS UNIT	
Takeda Katsuyori (commander)	200
Takeda Nobutomo (individual)	0
Takeda Nobumitsu	100
Mochizuki Nobumasa	60
Other named individuals	4
plus attendants to the above	728
Total	**1,092**

This is a much smaller number than the approximate figure of 3,000 given in the chronicles. However, the contingent from the Suruga sakikata-shu (239 horsemen) and the ashigaru-taisho (98 horsemen) are not allocated to a position in the records, so they may have formed part of the headquarters unit. There would also have been a considerable number of ashigaru. In addition, 360 horsemen remained behind in the siege lines. The overall formation chosen by the Takeda, with three forward divisions and one supporting them, was known by the poetic name of *kakuyoku* (crane's wing) from the shape of a crane's wings in flight.

For the majority of the Takeda troops their first sight of the enemy came only when they moved out of the woods to the east of Shidarahara.

RIGHT **Honda Tadakatsu was the loyal follower of Tokugawa Ieyasu, and the antlers on his helmet made him a prominent sight in the front ranks of the Oda/Tokugawa army at Nagashino. Much fierce fighting flowed around the section of the line commanded by Honda Tadakatsu. This statue of him is in the grounds of Okazaki castle.**

At the time of Nagashino Toyotomi Hideyoshi was in command of one of the three elite units who made up Oda Nobunaga's go *umamawari-shû*. He eventually succeeded Nobunaga as master of Japan when the latter was murdered, and became known to history as 'The Napoleon of Japan'.

From this point it was 200m at the narrowest to the Oda-Tokugawa line, and at its broadest, where Ichijô Nobutatsu was stationed, only 400m. Although he was aware of the number of guns that Oda Nobunaga possessed, two factors encouraged Takeda Katsuyori. The first was the heavy rain of the previous night, which was likely to have rendered the matchlocks unusable. The second was the likely speed of the Takeda charge. A distance of 200m would allow the Takeda to move quickly into a gallop as soon as they left the wooded area. With only 200m to cover, he could expect some casualties from bullets, but not enough to break the momentum of the charge. The horsemen would then be upon the hopeless ashigaru as they tried to reload, followed within seconds by the Takeda footsoldiers. There would then be a hand-to-hand fight in which the Oda guns would be a useless encumbrance. The Takeda samurai would sweep the fence to one side and pursue the retreating enemy down to the Toyokawa, where the river would cut off their retreat.

The Takeda Advance: 28 June, 06.00

One hour passed before Takeda Katsuyori gave the order to move forward. Most accounts of the battle of Nagashino give the impression that there was then a sudden charge which was broken by the gunfire, followed by another and another, until within minutes the majority of the Takeda horsemen lay dead from bullet wounds, and the Oda samurai finished them off. This is certainly the picture conveyed by the film *Kagemusha*, which takes many historical liberties with the battle. In fact, Takeda Katsuyori's order to advance set in motion no less than eight hours of bitter and bloody fighting. The matchlocks were decisive in producing the victory for Oda Nobunaga, but they were by no means the whole story. A good parallel is the battle of Agincourt, where the English longbows broke the French charge and created a situation which the English men at arms were able to exploit to their advantage.

At 06.00 on 28 June 1575 Takeda Katsuyori ordered the advance which began the Battle of Nagashino. To the sound of the Takeda war drums carried on the backs of ashigaru, the three vanguards of the Takeda cavalry under Yamagata, Naitô and Baba swept down from the hills onto the narrow fields. The initial move created considerable momentum. No guns opened up on them because Nobunaga's discipline was strict. The Takeda advance was then greatly slowed by the banks of the Rengogawa. Horses and men carefully negotiated the shallow river bed, picking up speed again as they mounted the far bank. At this point, with the horsemen within 50m of the fence, the volley firing began. As some gunfire had been expected the initial fall of men and horses did not cause Takeda Katsuyori any great concern. What shocked him was the rapid second volley, and then the third. All along the line his horsemen in the vanguards, and the attendant footsoldiers who had advanced with them, were falling in heaps as the fusillade tore into them from the calm Oda gunners under the iron hand of the men of the horô-shû.

It is this moment of the battle that is the most prominent feature of the famous painted screen depicting the battle of Nagashino in the Tokugawa Art Museum in Nagoya. Several incidents at different times of the day are shown on various parts of the screen, but the most dramatic vignette is of the ranks of Takeda horsemen falling beneath the bullets of the Oda matchlockmen. Although several personalities have been transposed from the positions they are believed to have occupied, the screen provides a vivid illustration of the impact of the matchlock volley firing. It was the three vanguard units who felt the first blast of the matchlockmen, but before looking at any section in detail, it is worth considering what the impact of the charge would have been from the point of view of the matchlockmen and their comrades – and for the Takeda cavalry.

The arquebuses used at Nagashino had a maximum range of 500m, a distance at which even volley firing could be expected to do little

Shibata Katsuie distinguished himself in every battle in which he took part. This print illustrates an incident during his defence of the castle of Chôkoji in 1570, when he smashed the water storage jars as earnest of his intentions to fight to the death. This so inspired the men under his command that they sallied out and carried all before them.

A rather elaborate print by Kuniyoshi depicting a samurai wielding a very large arquebus. The decisive weapons employed so successfully at Nagashino are likely to have been the smaller versions shown elsewhere in this book, with weapons like this one confined to use during the siege.

damage. The maximum effective range for causing casualties was 200m, which was just a little less than the distance from the fence to the woods out of which the Takeda cavalry began their charge. It is highly unlikely that Nobunaga would have allowed any firing at this range, because the slight wounds caused would not have interrupted the flow of the charge and would have wasted at least one of the volleys. At 50m, the distance from the fence to the Rengogawa, the effects would be more pronounced. Modern experiments have shown that an iron plate of 1mm thickness could have been be pierced by an arquebus ball at this distance, and as the iron from which the samurai's dô-maru armour was made was 0.8mm in thickness a hit from 50m range could have caused considerable damage. However, firing at 50 m was likely to be much less accurate than firing from 30m, because other modern experiments have shown that an experienced gunner could hit a man-sized target with five shots out of five at the shorter distance, compared with one in five at 50m. The first volley was therefore fired at a slow moving target, while the second was delivered at a potentially greater accuracy but at a moving target. The third volley must have been fired at almost point blank range.

There remains the question of how many volleys were actually fired. In a third modern experiment an experienced Japanese arquebus enthusiast managed to perform the sequence of load, prime, aim and fire in as little as fifteen seconds, a speed comparable to that of a flintlock musket. Other studies of arquebuses have shown that the need to keep the smouldering match out of the way while the pan is primed slows the process down to a more realistic rate of between twenty and thirty seconds, or in clumsy and inexperienced hands no better than one shot every minute. There is also the factor of the fouling of a barrel after a number of shots have been fired. In the case of an eighteenth century French flintlock, for example, fouling reduced the firing rate from one shot every twelve seconds to one shot every 45 seconds. As Nobunaga is recorded as having chosen his 'best shots' the rate of fire may well have be on the high side.

As we cannot know precisely the rate of fire used at Nagashino it is more profitable to approach the problem from the viewpoint of the Nagashino topography. In the Nagashino situation the gunners were being charged by horsemen capable of moving at 40km an hour or 11 metres per second. If the Rengogawa had not been in the way they would have been travelling at an uninterrupted speed and would therefore have covered the final 50m, during which we may assume all the firing took place, in about five seconds. The Rengogawa, however, must have slowed them to a walk, and at certain places brought them to a temporary halt. But even doubling or even trebling the time needed still only allows ten or fifteen seconds for the Oda army to shoot at them.

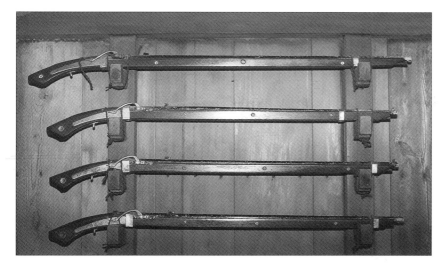

A rack of guns at Himeji castle. The arquebuses used at Nagashino would have been very similar in appearance to the guns shown here. One indirect effect of the battle of Nagashino was a concentration on means of defence, of which artillery in castles was but one illustration. The walkways round the interior of Himeji are furnished with racks for spears and guns.

This being the case, it is irrelevant whether the rate of fire was one shot every fifteen seconds or one shot every 45 seconds. We must instead envisage the three ranks of arquebusiers, all of whom already had loaded weapons, delivering only one shot each in that brief amount of time when the horsemen bore down upon them. As there were 3,000 gunners it means that some 8,000 bullets (misfires must have occurred) were delivered in three controlled volleys. It is possible that the carnage and confusion inflicted on the Takeda by the first two volleys may have given just enough time for the first rank to reload and fire a second volley of their own, making it four volleys in all, but a more likely scenario is that the process of reloading began en masse after the initial firing, and that

The little river known as the Rengogawa played a decisive strategic role at the battle of Nagashino. Its flow has now been controlled, as this photograph illustrates, but the viewer is still given a strong impression of how its banks would have slowed down a cavalry charge.

0600: **Baba Nobuharu, in command of the right wing, charges the fence after struggling across the Rengogawa**

1300: **Oda Nobunaga pulls his men back to the safety of the fences as the hand to hand fighting begins to go their way**

HEADING
1 Mizuno Nobumoto
2 Sakuma Nobumori
3 Niwa Nagahide
4 Oda Nobunaga
5 Hashiba Hideyoshi
6 Takigawa Kazumasu
7 Torii Mototada
8 Tokugawa Nobuyasu
9 Ishikawa Kazumasa
10 Tokugawa Ieyasu
11 Honda Takakatsu
12 Sakakibara Yasumasa
13 Osuka Yasutaka
14 Sakai Tadatsugu
15 Okubo Tadayo

ODA NOBUNAGA

TOKUGAWA IEYASU

N

THE CHARGE, 28 JUNE 1575
As dawn broke over Shidarahara, Oda Nobunaga made his final dispositions and the four Takeda divisions began to advance against him.

0600: **Positioned within sight of the Oda line, Takeda Katsuyori orders the vanguard to attack**

0600: **The main bodies of the three forward units attack**

0900: **Takeda Katsuyori commits his reserves and his headquarters unit**

0600: **The vanguard units (centre - Naito Masatoyo; left - Yamagata Masakage) charge the fence after crossing the Rengogawa**

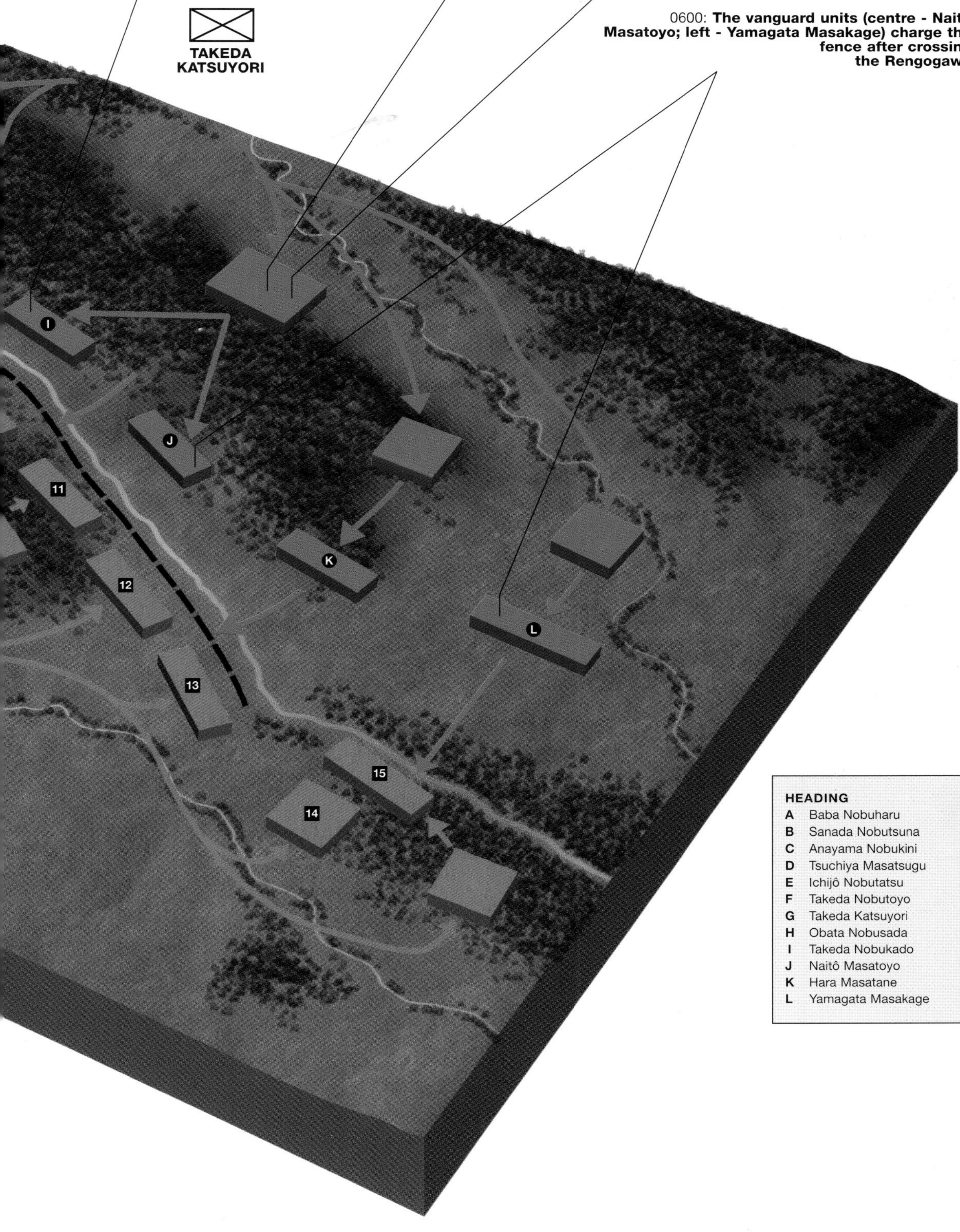

TAKEDA
KATSUYORI

I

J

11

12

13

15

14

K

L

HEADING	
A	Baba Nobuharu
B	Sanada Nobutsuna
C	Anayama Nobukini
D	Tsuchiya Masatsugu
E	Ichijô Nobutatsu
F	Takeda Nobutoyo
G	Takeda Katsuyori
H	Obata Nobusada
I	Takeda Nobukado
J	Naitô Masatoyo
K	Hara Masatane
L	Yamagata Masakage

The fence on Shidarahara as seen from the Rengogawa, about 50 metres away. This was the sight that would have met the eyes of the Takeda horsemen as they negotiated the Rengogawa and spurred their horses on up the slope towards the palisade.

the three ranks did not fire again until the next wave of horsemen arrived at the Rengogawa. This is certainly indicated by the fact that the whole battle lasted eight hours. Nagashino was definitely not the 'machine-gun' battle that is erroneously implied by the film *Kagemusha*.

So what happened to the arquebusiers after they had fired? In spite of all the noise, confusion and danger they would have had to give their total concentration to the business of reloading, ensuring that the touch hole was clear, that the bullet was correctly rammed down, and that there was no chance of the smouldering match causing a premature discharge. Here the presence of the fence and their ashigaru comrades with their 5.6m long spears would have provided the protection they needed in this Japanese version of a European 'pike and shot' unit.

It would also be a mistake to think of mounted samurai charging forwards and simply crashing into a line of infantry, whether or not they were protected by fences. The success of a cavalry charge depended on the footsoldiers breaking ranks, at which the horsemen could enter their midst and cut them down at will. This had happened in the European theatre of war in 1568 at the battle of Riberac. The point about Nobunaga's tactics was that the arrangement of the guns, the fences and the spearmen allowed him to control the impact of the Takeda assault. As an English commentator put it in 1593, 'the charge of horsemen against shot ... is mortall if they be not either garded with pikes, or have the vantage of ditches, or hedges, or woods, where they cannot reach them.'

No doubt the dismounted samurai of the Oda and Tokugawa would have been itching to join in the fight, but it is probable that any such combats at this stage of the battle only occurred against any Takeda cavalryman who had passed through the gaps in the fence. These gaps allowed the creation of a 'killing-ground' for such separated horsemen, who would become the prey both for samurai swords and ashigaru spears. Should any of the Oda samurai have ventured out from the fences it is likely that they would have been speedily recalled. Their time of glory was to come later. To add to the defence from palisade and spear quite dense clouds of smoke would also have been expected, a factor I saw illustrated dramatically when I observed arquebuses being fired at Nagashino in the annual festival in 1986.

The ideal situation for the Oda/Tokugawa army would therefore have been that the defensive measures outlined above would have given the arquebus corps sufficient time to prepare for three more volleys as the next wave of horsemen charged in. Subsequent events indicate that this ideal state was actually achieved, as successive mounted attacks suffered hundreds more mounted casualties.

Tobigasuyama: 28 June, 08.00

While Takeda Katsuyori's vanguard units were thoroughly engaged in the advance that they thought would sweep the Oda and Tokugawa armies off the field, a rear attack was taking place far behind them. It is unlikely that the Takeda army who charged the guns were aware until after the battle was over that Sakai Tadatsugu had launched his attack on Takeda Nobuzane's forts of Tobigasuyama at 08.00. In complete secrecy Sakai Tadatsugu divided his unit into three sections. The first attacked the fort of Nakayama with such force that the defenders abandoned it for Tobigasu, which Sakai Tadatsugu's other two divisions attacked in the ensuing confusion. Both attacks were begun with matchlock fire from the 500 gunners under Kanamori Nagachika, followed by the shooting of fire arrows onto the temporary buildings, whose thatched roofs soon caught light. There was then a charge into the compound by the samurai. The commander, Takeda Nobuzane, was killed in the fierce hand-to-hand fighting which ensued. Soon smoke was seen rising from

Looking from the fence across the plain of Shidarahara to the woods which divided the battlefield of Nagashino from the castle. This was the view that would have tested the mettle of Oda Nobunaga's three thousand gunners as 12,000 horsemen emerged from the trees and came galloping towards them

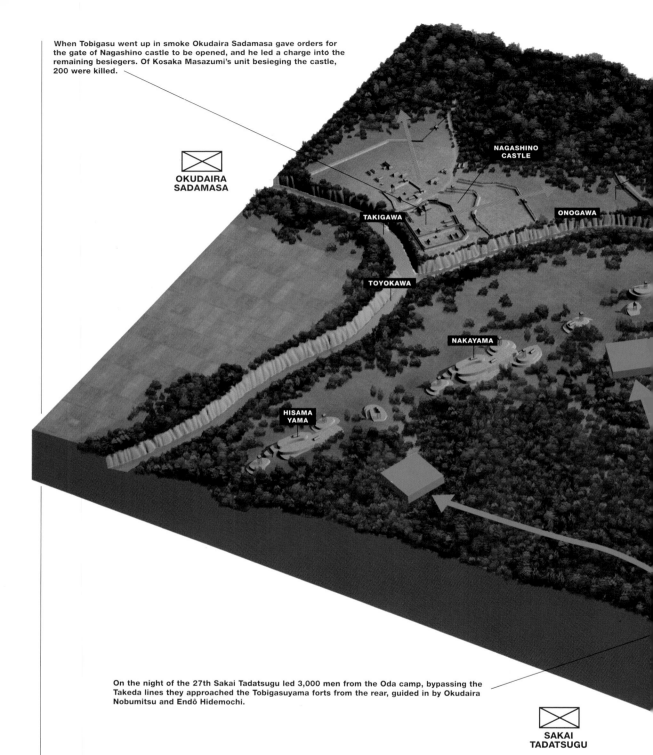

When Tobigasu went up in smoke Okudaira Sadamasa gave orders for the gate of Nagashino castle to be opened, and he led a charge into the remaining besiegers. Of Kosaka Masazumi's unit besieging the castle, 200 were killed.

OKUDAIRA
SADAMASA

NAGASHINO
CASTLE

ONOGAWA

TAKIGAWA

TOYOKAWA

NAKAYAMA

HISAMA
YAMA

On the night of the 27th Sakai Tadatsugu led 3,000 men from the Oda camp, bypassing the Takeda lines they approached the Tobigasuyama forts from the rear, guided in by Okudaira Nobumitsu and Endō Hidemochi.

SAKAI
TADATSUGU

THE TOBIGASU RAID, 0800 28 JUNE 1575

Having been given permission by Oda Nobunaga, Sakai Tadatsugu leads a force of men against the Takeda siege lines on the hill of Tobigasu.

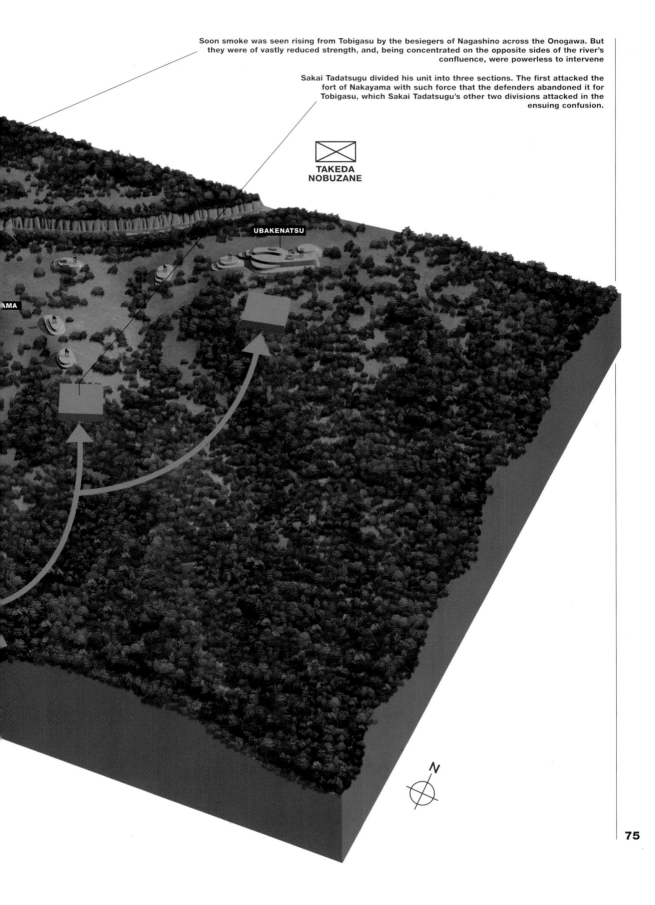

Soon smoke was seen rising from Tobigasu by the besiegers of Nagashino across the Onogawa. But they were of vastly reduced strength, and, being concentrated on the opposite sides of the river's confluence, were powerless to intervene

Sakai Tadatsugu divided his unit into three sections. The first attacked the fort of Nakayama with such force that the defenders abandoned it for Tobigasu, which Sakai Tadatsugu's other two divisions attacked in the ensuing confusion.

TAKEDA NOBUZANE

UBAKENATSU

...AMA

N

Tobigasu by the besiegers of Nagashino across the Onogawa. But they were of vastly reduced strength and concentrated on the opposite sides of the river's confluence, and so were powerless to intervene, all they could do was watch as one section of their army was annihilated

The chaos on Tobigasu had also been spotted by Okudaira Sadamasa and the garrison of Nagashino. They had long been aware that the bulk of the Takeda army had moved away. The noise from Shidarahara must have reached them, and when Tobigasu went up in smoke Okudaira Sadamasa gave orders for the gate of Nagashino castle to be opened, and he led a charge into the remaining besiegers. This sally is illustrated on the Nagashino screen. Further destruction of the Takeda army ensued, and in spite of the castle garrison being weakened from hunger and illness, they inflicted great damage on the besiegers. Of Kôsaka Masazumi's unit besieging the castle, 200 were killed. The Tokugawa force lost one high-ranking samurai in the sally. He was Matsudaira Koretada, one of Okudaira's two assistant commanders.

Shidarahara: 28 June, 09.00

Back at Shidarahara the attack on the Oda-Tokugawa line had now been continuing for three hours, and still the fence held, but the actual nature of combat varied from place to place. In the centre there was a straightforward fight between Takeda Nobukado's and Naitô Masatoyo's units and the Oda line, which held them in check in spite of repeated brave charges. We may perhaps envisage a series of rushes intended to break the gunners' resolve, but as successive charges had to pick their way through the bodies of their comrades, the impetus soon passed to the defenders.

Over on the right wing the vanguard under Baba Nobuharu was experiencing great difficulty in coming to grips with the enemy, and

suffering casualties as they did so. The densely forested hill to the right prevented any outflanking movement and served to funnel the charging horsemen into the gap. As Baba's vanguard withdrew to rest they were replaced by the Sanada brothers, Tsuchiya Masatsugu, Ichijô Nobutatsu and Anayama Nobukimi. Again the matchlock balls tore into them. Tsuchiya Masatsugu was shot dead. Sanada Nobutsuna and Nobuteru lost 200 men to the firing but then managed to break through into the Oda lines where they engaged in hand-to-hand combat with Shibata Katsuie and Hashiba Hideyoshi, but both the Sanada brothers were killed. However, at this point Baba Nobuharu returned to the fray, determined to break through the fence towards Nobunaga's headquarters. Here Sakuma Nobumori held the high ground, and as Baba Nobuharu advanced, he ordered a fake retreat. This drew the Takeda men on into the 'killing zone'. They occupied the hill with great elation, and then proceeded to attack the next stockade from the side. However, Shibata Katsuie and Hashiba Hideyoshi had been prepared for such an eventuality, and attacked them in the flank and rear, driving them off with many casualties. Out of 700 men in his vanguard, Baba Nobuharu now had only 80 left.

The right wing of the Oda army was not protected by a fence, and in front of Okubo Tadayo was the veteran Yamagata Masakage, aged 60. Their encounter is well illustrated on the Nagashino screen. Okubo Tadayo has a sashimono of a large golden disc, while his younger brother, Okubo Tadasuke, wears a sashimono of a golden butterfly. They had fought the Takeda at the Battle of Mikata-ga-hara, and were under no illusions as to the task which was required of them. Unhindered by

The Takeda attack on the palisade was launched to the sound of war drums carried on the backs of ashigaru. Another ashigaru would walk behind to beat it. This example is preserved in the museum on the site of Nagashino castle, and the caption proudly proclaims that it carries bloodstains from the battle.

fences, and with a wider ground over which to operate than their comrades along the line, the Yamagata vanguard, with Masakage at their head, took casualties from the bullets and crashed into the Okubo body of troops. Here a fierce hand-to-hand fight developed as the first mêlée of the day, so we may envisage the Okubo ranks parting to allow the horsemen in. From this moment on the matchlock fire would only have been sporadic, as this area of the battlefield became one huge hacking mass of men and horses. The samurai sought single combat. The attendants tried to protect their lords, while the ashigaru spearmen and gunners lashed out at any they could see who were identified as enemy. As he had already demonstrated outside the walls of Yoshida, Yamagata Masakage was skilled in single combat, and still had the assistance of the three samurai who had attended him then. Yamagata must have stayed on his horse, because we then read of him breaking free from the mêlée and leading his men in a charge against the unit of Honda Tadakatsu. He was met with a hail of bullets and finally shot from his horse's back. As he fell, an unknown samurai ran up and cut off his head, which was taken back in triumph.

At about this moment Takeda Katsuyori ordered a general attack along the line with all the reserves and his own bodyguard. He rode behind the unit of Takeda Nobutoyo in the centre, led by his vanguard under Mochizuki Nobumasa and followed by his rearguard under Takeda Nobumitsu. Yet even this brave attempt with fresh troops made no impact of the Oda-Tokugawa lines. So the battle continued as the

Three gunners line up at Nagashino. This 'firing line' from the Nagashino festival gives a good idea of what may have been the appearance of the gunners at Nagashino, standing or kneeling shoulder to shoulder behind the wooden palisade. The firing of reproduction matchlocks is a well respected activity in Japan, and the club from Yonezawa represented here are much in demand for historical re-enactments

morning wore on. In spite of the vast scale of the slaughter and the anonymity of many encounters, the chroniclers still found space to record certain individual feats of samurai heroism. In an isolated incident, Honda Shigetsugu of the Tokugawa force launched a single-handed attack on seven or eight enemy horsemen and killed two in spite of being wounded in seven places himself. Elsewhere, a retainer of Torii Mototada called Nagata Hatsumi-no-suke took the head of an anonymous samurai whose sashimono flag bore the characters '*ni gatsu*' (February). After the battle he discovered that he had taken the head of an important leader called Mochizuki Nobumasa, who was Katsuyori's cousin and commanded 60 horsemen in the goshinrui-shû.

Shidarahara: 28 June, 13.00

The hand-to-hand fighting continued until about 13.00. At this point Oda Nobunaga gave orders for the blowing of the *horagai*, the shell trumpets that were the pre-arranged signal for his army to withdraw into the line of the fences. Temporarily disengaged from their enemies, the Takeda began to retreat in the direction of the Hôrai-ji temple on the road back towards Kai province and safety. Seeing this movement, Oda Nobunaga ordered a pursuit. The Oda and Tokugawa samurai mounted up and rode out from the palisade. The first prominent person to be caught was the commander of the vanguard of the centre squadron, the veteran Naitô Masatoyo, who was accompanied by the 100 men left out of his initial command of 1,000. He was apprehended by Honda Tadakatsu, Osuga Yasutaka and Sakakibara Yasumasa, who had with them a number of ashigaru archers. They fired at Masatoyo, hitting him many times. He fell from his horse, and seeing him trying to lift his spear, a samurai called

LEFT Takeda Katsuyori leads his contingent into battle. In this section from a modern copy of the Nagashino screen Takeda Katsuyori is distinguished by the Japanese character meaning 'great' on his standard. During the battle Katsuyori commanded from a hill overlooking the battlefield, and only joined in the fighting when he committed his reserves.

79

A gunner at the ready at Nagashino. Every year, on the anniversary of the battle, a major festival is held at Hôrai, centring on the castle site itself. Details of the arquebus may be seen in this picture of one of the gunners at the 1986 celebration. The matchlockmen at the battle were ashigaru, and would therefore not have worn such elaborate armour.

Asahina Yasukatsu thrust a spear at him and took his head. Masatoyo was 52 years old.

The most heroic death during the withdrawal was suffered by the other great veteran Baba Nobuharu. He took it upon himself to ensure Takeda Katsuyori's safety by covering his retreat. When the Oda forces caught up with his rearguard unit, Baba Nobuharu announced his name in the manner of the samurai of old, stressing that only the greatest of samurai would take his head. The challenge was answered by two samurai, who attacked him simultaneously with their spears, and soon his head was off his body. He was 62 years old.

Takeda Katsuyori withdrew into his mountains, accompanied at the last by only two samurai retainers, Tsuchiya Masatsune, brother of the other Tsuchiya killed at Nagashino, and Hajikano Masatsugu. Swift messengers had already conveyed the grim news to Tsutsuji-ga-saki, and Katsuyori was met en route by Kosaka Masanobu, who had abandoned his campaign against the Uesugi and hurried down to safeguard Katsuyori's entry into Kai. The appearance of this force on the border set a limit to Nobunaga's pursuit, and Katsuyori escaped.

Takeda Katsuyori left behind him on the battlefield 10,000 dead out of a total Takeda army of 15,000, a casualty rate of 67 per cent. The losses were particularly acute among the upper ranks of the Takeda retainers and family members. These were the men who had led from the front and charged into the Oda-Tokugawa lines at the head of their followers. Out of 97 named samurai leaders at Nagashino, including generals of ashigaru, flag commissioners and samurai commanders in the goshinrui-shû and the fudai-karo-shû, 54 were killed and two badly wounded - 56 per cent of the total. No fewer than eight of the veteran Takeda 'Twenty Four Generals', the men of Shingen's generation, lay dead: Hara Masatane, Sanada Nobutsuna, Saigusa Moritomo, Naitô Masatoyo, Yamagata Masakage, Tsuchiya Masatsugu and Baba Nobuharu. Losses on the allied side were also quite heavy – 6,000 killed out of 38,000, a rate of 16 per cent – but this did not compare to the tragedy of the Takeda that bore the name of Nagashino.

AFTERMATH

The Destruction of Takeda Katsuyori

After such an overwhelming victory as Nagashino, it is perhaps surprising to note that the final defeat of Takeda Katsuyori did not occur until 1582. Following the battle he withdrew to Kai and maintained a defensive policy for the rest of his life. Kai and Shinano were easier to defend than the coastal provinces of Mikawa and Tôtômi, and the Takeda strategic position was also greatly helped by the death in 1578 of their great rival Uesugi Kenshin. The latter's demise was so fortunate for all concerned that ninja were suspected, and following his death a succession dispute within the Uesugi family took a lot of pressure off the Takeda from this direction.

The Takeda strategy was now one of pure defence and survival. Tokugawa Ieyasu continued to harass them, and between 1575 and 1581 he conducted a series of operations against Katsuyori, which resulted in the regaining of Takatenjin Castle, lost before Nagashino. By this time even Katsuyori's own subjects were beginning to lose confidence in him, and in 1581 he alienated many by building a new castle at Shimpu near Nirasaki, proclaiming it as his new capital. Shingen had never relied on a fortified place as his capital. Tsutsuji-ga-saki, his headquarters in Kofu, had been a one-storey mansion complex with just one moat. Now his heir, who had failed at Nagashino, was seeking refuge behind stone walls.

The following year one of the major Takeda vassals revolted. This was Kiso Yoshimasa, who held the castle of Kiso-Fukushima on the

The warrior in the foreground of this picture is Baba Nobuharu, one of Takeda Katsuyori's ablest generals, who was killed during the retreat. As Baba Nobuharu covered Katsuyori's withdrawal he was challenged by two samurai. Nobuharu proclaimed his name and pedigree in the manner of a samurai of old, and was cut down. Behind him is Saigusa Moritomo, who was also killed at Nagashino.

81

This early print by Kuniyoshi, which is not of Nagashino, illustrates the effect of arquebus fire on the human body. The victim is a certain Yamanaka Dankuro, of whom no other details are known. The overcoming of the sword by the gun is a theme regarded as tragic by several samurai commentators.

Nakasendô, which was almost at the limit of Takeda territory. Encouraged by such dissension, in 1582 the combined forces of Oda and Tokugawa turned against the Takeda. Oda Nobutada, Nobunaga's son, invaded Shinano, and one by one the Takeda allies collapsed before them. Even Anayama Nobukimi, who had been one of Shingen's Twenty-Four Generals and survived Nagashino, left Katsuyori for the winning side.

Only his closest relatives now stood by him. His younger brother Morinobu, who had been adopted into the Nishina family, held out valiantly at Takatô Castle, along the route which the great Shingen had taken to his victory at Mikata-ga-hara. Then Ieyasu struck northwards into Kai, and the Takeda resistance collapsed. As the Tokugawa approached, Takeda Katsuyori burned his new castle of Shimpu and fled to the most distant mountains of his territory. Oyamada Nobushige, one of the old Twenty-Four who had stayed in the siege lines during the Battle of Nagashino, had offered him refuge in his castle of Iwadono, but when Katsuyori arrived, he found the gates shut against him.

By now his army had shrunk to 300 men. The only famous name from the original Twenty-Four Generals who remained with him to the last was the family of Tsuchiya. The three sons of Tsuchiya Masatsugu joined Katsuyori and his son Nobukatsu at their last battle at Torii-bata, a pass overlooked by a mountain called Temmoku-zan, by which name the battle is usually known. There were 30 survivors. As the Tsuchiya brothers held the enemy back Katsuyori's young wife, aged 19, committed suicide by stabbing herself. Katsuyori, acting as her second, cut off her head, then with his son committed hara-kiri. The head of Takeda Katsuyori was sent to Oda Nobunaga for his inspection. 'The right eye was closed, and the left eye was enlivened with a scowl.' wrote a

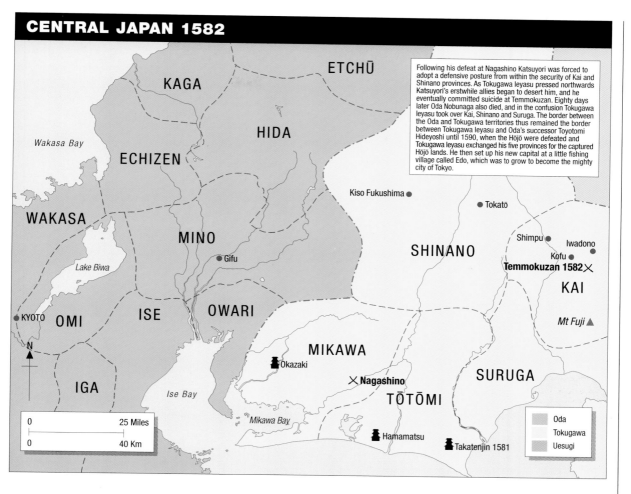

ETCHŪ

KAGA

HIDA

Wakasa Bay

ECHIZEN

WAKASA

MINO

Lake Biwa

Gifu

KYOTO

OMI   ISE   OWARI

N

IGA

Ise Bay

0   25 Miles
0   40 Km

Mikawa Bay

Kiso Fukushima •

Tokatō •

SHINANO

Shimpu •   Iwadono •
Kofu •
Temmokuzan 1582 ✕

KAI

Mt Fuji ▲

MIKAWA

Okazaki

✕ **Nagashino**

TŌTOMI

SURUGA

Hamamatsu

Takatenjin 1581

Following his defeat at Nagashino Katsuyori was forced to adopt a defensive posture from within the security of Kai and Shinano provinces. As Tokugawa Ieyasu pressed northwards Katsuyori's erstwhile allies began to desert him, and he eventually committed suicide at Temmokuzan. Eighty days later Oda Nobunaga also died, and in the confusion Tokugawa Ieyasu took over Kai, Shinano and Suruga. The border between the Oda and Tokugawa territories thus remained the border between Tokugawa Ieyasu and Oda's successor Toyotomi Hideyoshi until 1590, when the Hōjō were defeated and Tokugawa Ieyasu exchanged his five provinces for the captured Hōjō lands. He then set up his new capital at a little fishing village called Edo, which was to grow to become the mighty city of Tokyo.

	Oda
	Tokugawa
	Uesugi

chronicler, 'Nobunaga was moved to tears at the sight of the head of the great commander. All agreed that Nobunaga may have been victorious in battle, but was defeated by the head of Katsuyori.' So died the unfortunate Takeda Katsuyori, the man who had supposedly been born as a act of revenge by a fox disguised as a beautiful woman. He is buried within walking distance of the place where he died, a tragic figure in Japanese history, the heir who inherited his father's mantle but showed himself to be unworthy of it.

Military lessons of Nagashino

The Battle of Nagashino holds a unique place in Japanese history. The siege which preceded it is regarded as one of the three classic sieges of Japan, but it was the skilful manner in which Oda Nobunaga secured his victory which has earned Nagashino such a reputation. As noted earlier, Oda Nobunaga applied on a large scale the important lessons he had learned from years of fighting against a fanatic army composed almost entirely of lower class footsoldiers, who fought like samurai and compensated for their lack of skill in the traditional samurai weaponry by investing heavily in matchlock guns.

Nobunaga's first achievement at Nagashino was to make a correct assessment of his enemy. He knew their skills, their strengths and their

LEFT **Bitter hand to hand fighting is shown in this section of a painted scroll preserved in the local museum, the Nagashino Castle Preservation Hall. Two warriors on the right, identified only as 'Nobunaga's troops' press home their attack against Takeda Katsuyori and his loyal supporters at his last battle in 1582.**

83

weaknesses, and had suffered defeat at their hands at Mikata-ga-hara. Their strength was their cavalry, but their weakness was that they would use their cavalry unadvisedly. The mere fact that Takeda Katsuyori planned to attack him, rather than use Nagashino for a defensive position, was evidence enough of the latter.

Nobunaga's brilliant additions to the earlier situation he had experienced at Ishiyama Hongan-ji were threefold. The first was the creation of simple field fortifications, which were just sufficient to give the matchlockmen the protection and confidence they needed. This was combined with a sensible choice of ground. He opted to stand against the Takeda not on the hills directly overlooking the castle, where all their movements would easily be seen, but one range back, where the little Rengogawa would play a decisive role as a moat. The final factor was the rigid discipline supplied by his most trusted individual warriors from his bodyguard, who had loyalty only to him and did not have the responsibility of controlling their own units of troops. Oda Nobunaga thus produced a formula that was calculated to withstand the Takeda assault, and it worked perfectly. It was not a total victory in that it did not completely destroy the Takeda clan in one day, but it came very close to it, and the shock produced in Kofu by the returning wounded must have been tremendous.

There is some evidence that the experience of Nagashino produced something of a defensive mentality among other daimyô for years to come. This is shown by the subsequent behaviour of certain samurai generals who were present at Nagashino. In 1583 Toyotomi Hideyoshi fought and defeated Sakuma Nobumori at the Battle of Shizugatake, when the latter was in the process of besieging a castle. A rapid march by Hideyoshi's army caught Sakuma unprepared with no fence for protection. One year later Hideyoshi prepared to fight Tokugawa Ieyasu in the area of Komaki castle. Both were veterans of Nagashino, and both

Hand to hand fighting is shown in this section from the *Ehon Taikô-ki*. The gunners at Nagashino broke the impact of the cavalry charge, and offered the samurai up for bitter and to hand fighting beside the palisade lines. This part of the battle lasted for the whole of the morning. Spears and swords were the common weapons used.

This print by Yoshitoshi, which is concerned with one of the battles of the wars of Restoration in the 19th century, nonetheless conveys the feeling of swathes of samurai laid low by a hail of bullets. Interestingly, the victims include a drum carrier, whose drum bears the Takeda mon of four lozenges.

prepared extensive defence lines and earthworks. A stalemate ensued, and was only broken when Hideyoshi sent an army to attack Mikawa province, which one suspects had as much to do with relieving boredom as any grand strategy. The resulting battle of Nagakute, fought far from the lines, was a pitched samurai battle in the grand manner.

The experience of Nagashino certainly encouraged all daimyô to obtain more firearms, and as numbers increased, the advantage which Nobunaga had enjoyed was unlikely to be repeated. The situation of Nagashino was also difficult to recreate. A decline in mounted warfare may also be noted, so that at the final battle of the siege of Osaka castle in 1615, Tokugawa Ieyasu ordered his samurai to leave their horses at the rear and go in on foot with their spears.

There is, however, a persistent impression that the use of firearms was not really regarded as part of the glorious samurai tradition, and when peace came with the triumph of the Tokugawa, it was the samurai sword which became the cult weapon and badge of the samurai class, not the matchlock gun, in spite of the large number of the latter in the Tokugawa armoury.

The Fate of the Nagashino Commanders

The victor of Nagashino, Oda Nobunaga, was only to survive Takeda Katsuyori by a few months. He was murdered in 1582 by one of his own generals and was succeeded by Toyotomi Hideyoshi, who avenged his master with consummate opportunism. Following his successful command of the castle, Okudaira Sadamasa received the unusual honour of being presented by Oda Nobunaga with one of the syllables out of his name, so that he became known as Okudaira Nobumasa. He also received from Tokugawa Ieyasu considerable lands, a sword, and his daughter in marriage. Okudaira Nobumasa continued to serve Ieyasu, and took part in the final campaign against Katsuyori in 1582. He died in 1615. Tokugawa Ieyasu, of course, achieved the prize which had eluded Takeda Shingen, Takeda Katsuyori and Oda Nobunaga when he became Shogun in 1603, all rivals having been vanquished.

As for the castle of Nagashino, its days were numbered as a vital strategic fortress. The defeat of Katsuyori had been so catastrophic that it was highly unlikely that he would ever return to Mikawa by that route, so in 1576 the site was abandoned, and apart from the Iida railway line has remained as a rocky bluff above a fast flowing river to this day.

SELECT BIBLIOGRAPHY

For those who are skilled in the Japanese language, the best modern history of the battle is *Nagashino no tatakai* by Kenichi Futaki in the series Rekishi Gunzo – Kassen Dokiyumento Vol 1. (Gakken Mook 1989, Book code: 62534-77). There is a wealth of detail, including full lists of participants. Also recommended is *Shiro to Kassen: Nagashino no tatakai to Shimabara no Ran*, by various authors, in the series Rekishi o yomi naosu Vol. 15 (Asahi Shimbunsha 1993, Book Code: 61381-01), which includes superb reconstructed drawings of Nagashino and the Shimabara revolt of 1638, and a full-colour reproduction of the Nagashino screen.

For books in English, readers will find much extra useful information about warfare during the 'Period of Warring States' in my comprehensive work *The Samurai Sourcebook* (Cassell 1998). My earlier book, *The Samurai, A Military History*, was reprinted as a paperback in 1995, but unfortunately does not include the photograph of the Nagashino Screen that appeared in the hardback edition. *Samurai: The Warrior Tradition* (Cassell 1996) contains colour plates of the Takeda heraldry, while *Samurai Warfare* (Cassell 1996) has detailed case studies of samurai battles and many colour illustrations.

For a regular monthly update on samurai matters please visit my website at:

http://freespace.virgin.net/stephen.turnbull/publications.htm

As well as the latest news about my own most recent research and publications you will find reviews of new books, computer games, wargaming, public lectures and museum exhibitions. You can also use the website to send me feedback about my books.

The highly entertaining film *Kagemusha* tells a fictionalised version of the story of the downfall of the Takeda family under Katsuyori. Most of the film is quite superb, and is only let down by the final scene, which is the battle of Nagashino. Almost all the details of the battle are sadly wrong. It is fought on a wide open plain. Katsuyori's decision to attack is made to look even more nonsensical than it actually was, and the carnage inflicted by the arquebus corps acting alone would make one think that they were using Maxim guns. Apart from this the film paints a magnificent picture of samurai warfare that is only equalled by Kurosawa's other colour masterpiece *Ran*, and must be viewed by anyone who has read this book.

THE BATTLEFIELD TODAY

The Nagashino battlefield is one of the best preserved of all Japanese battlefields, and very rewarding to visit. The best time to go is May, when the Nagashino Kassen Nobori Matsuri (Battle of Nagashino Banner Festival) is held in the grounds of the castle. There is usually a performance of the firing of reproduction matchlocks.

All the major sites near Nagashino may be reached conveniently by rail. The Kodama service of the Shinkansen 'Bullet Train' stops at Toyohashi, from where a train connects to Toyokawa. At Toyokawa a change is necessary on to the Iida line, a single track railway that traverses the battlefield. The stop for Nagashino castle is Nagashino-jô. From here it is a short walk to the site of the castle. The hon-maru is preserved as a grassy area, and there is an excellent museum, the Nagashino Castle Preservation Hall. The exhibits include a fine collection of arms and armour, and a blood-stained drum used in the battle. To see the classic view of the castle site from across the river's confluence it is necessary to walk upstream and double back on the other side of the Onogawa. It is also possible to walk down a path to the river and appreciate the steep cliffs of the Yagyû-guruwa.

From further up the Onogawa a walk may be made up to the summit of Tobigasuyama, where the surprise attack was launched by Sakai Tadatsugu. This hill gives the finest view of the castle site, taking in the Arumi area across the river, where Torii Sune'emon was crucified, and a panoramic view of what was the entire castle area, leading up to Daitsûjiyama and the Buddhist Daitsû-ji at its foot. Takeda Katsuyori's headquarters on Iojiyama is well preserved. The Io-ji at its foot contains a small museum, with one or two items relating to the battle. A footpath leads up to the site of Katsuyori's base, but trees obstruct the view from there. On the south side of the hill another footpath leads down through the area occupied by Anayama and others, but again the view of the castle is obscured, this time by building developments.

Shidarahara may be reached by taking the train and getting off two stations down the line back to Toyokawa. Here it is a five minute walk to the centre of the battlefield, where the local council of Shinshiro town has erected a replica of the famous fence. The topography of the area is almost unchanged since 1575, and the distances that the Takeda horsemen had to traverse, as well as the obstacle the Rengogawa presented, can be easily appreciated. Near the site is a new museum, opened in 1997 which contains many items of interest. The sites of Noda and Yoshida castles may also be visited, but there is little to see at either. One of the most historic and beautiful sights in the vicinity is the temple of Hôrai-ji, set at the foot of a huge cliff. Takeda Shingen was taken to the Hôrai-ji when he was shot at Noda, and it later provided a temporary refuge for those escaping from the battlefield of Nagashino.

A visit to Temmoku-zan, the site of Takeda Katsuyori's last stand, involves a long but enjoyable journey up into the mountains to the north of Mount Fuji. A local train from Kofu stops at Enzan, where Shingen is buried, and there is a magnificent museum containing the old Takeda flags and many other military treasures. The train continues to Hajikano, where it is a walk of about a mile to Torii-bata and Katsuyori's grave at the Keitoku-In. A festival in his honour is held here in April. In Kofu in April there is a march past of an army of people dressed in the costume of the Takeda samurai, while at nearby Isawa Spa one can witness the re-fighting of the battle of Kawanakajima, carried out by hundreds of enthusiastic students in armour with the Takeda flags that would have been worn at Nagashino.

The Hôrai-ji temple, which lies at the foot of a steep cliff just behind Nagashino. The Hôrai-ji was the place to which Takeda Shingen was taken after he received his mortal wound at the siege of Noda, and after the battle of Nagashino his son and heir, Takeda Katsuyori, sought respite here during his desperate retreat back to Kai. The temple has given its name to the modern town that includes the site of Nagashino.

WARGAMING THE CAMPAIGN AND BATTLE OF NAGASHINO
by Arthur Harman

In the long term, Tokugawa Ieyasu was the real victor of Nagashino. His territories had suffered the raid by Takeda Katsuyori which led to the siege of Nagashino, and his Mikawa samurai greatly distinguished themselves in the subsequent batle. It was Tokugawa troops who led the assault in 1582 on the Takeda territories, which then became Tokugawa possessions, giving him the service of the renowned Takeda fighting men, and their equally renowned gold mines. He became Shogun in 1603.

Whenever an historical campaign or battle is to be recreated as a wargame the first decision that must be taken is whether to allow the players freedom of action, or to structure the game in such a way that they must abide by the strategic and tactical choices of the original commanders. If players have freedom of action, however carefully their briefings have been written, the game invariably fails to follow the exact historical sequence of events, and there is no reason to suppose that a wargame of the Nagashino Campaign will be any different. Who, after reading this book, would choose to send cavalry against a palisade held by ashigaru matchlockmen? This appendix will, therefore, suggest a variety of games, which may be played either in isolation or as part of a series, in which the players cannot reverse the most significant decisions taken by the original commanders, but must operate within those constraints, so as to recreate – insofar as any wargame can hope to do – the atmosphere of the historical sequence of events.

Invasion of Mikawa

Takeda Katsuyori's invasion of Mikawa province may be recreated as a wargame using one of two very different structures.

The first is a conventional kriegsspiel in which each of the players has a personal copy of a detailed map of the theatre of operations, upon which to plan the manoeuvres of his troops, and gives written notes of his personal actions, orders and messages to other played characters and subordinate comanders, to an umpire or umpires. It is the umpires who will determine, on their master map, out of the players' sight and earshot, whether and after how long orders or messages reach other players, when and how orders are implemented by non-played characters and when contact is made between opposing forces. They will decide what degree of knowledge the rival daimyôs should be given of events outside their immediate field of vision and report back to them accordingly. Such a game is said to be 'closed' because the players will be given, for example, no information of forces or events about which the umpires decide their characters would of have been unaware in reality, and do not administer any rules governing movement or combat themselves.

The second, the Matrix Game, developed by Chris Engle of the United States, is an 'open' game, in which all players and an umpire sit around one map of the area and the former take it in turns to propose Arguments, comprising of an Action and three Reasons why a desired Result of that Action should ensue, before the assembled company. Arguments, unlike the orders in a kriegsspiel, may apply not just to one's own troops, but to hostile forces or to natural phenomena, such as the weather, although some umpires prefer to forbid players to make Arguments concerning forces or events of which their characters would, in reality, be unaware. The umpire, using a few simple principles and die

The suicide of Takeda Katsuyori. A section from the painted scroll in the Nagashino Castle museum shows Takeda Katsuyori committing *hara-kiri* as Oda Nobunaga's troops approach. Note how he has stripped off his body armour to allow himself to perform the deed unrestricted. The artist has depicted in a very graphic manner the moment when the abdomen is opened.

rolls, will decide whether, and to what extent, an Argument succeeds and resolve conflicts between opposing Arguments, inform all players of the various outcomes and update the map where necessary.

A Matrix Game, albeit not so realistic in structure, is a more sociable entertainment than a kriegsspiel, and thus ideal for light-hearted recreational play, and to generate tactical contacts which may be transferred to a tabletop to be fought out as battles with model soldiers. One could envisage a Matrix Game of the Nagashino campaign in which the players, dressed in suitable garments to suggest samurai costume, sat cross-legged on the floor, drinking tea or sake, around a specially drawn map, decorated in the Japanese style with characters and illustrations, upon which counters or bodies of small-scale troops, bearing appropriately coloured sashimono banners to identify their commanders.

Whichever of these two structures is chosen, the game will begin when Takeda Katsuyori, having invaded Mikawa province in the belief that Oga Yashiro would betray Okazaki castle to him, learns that the plot has been discovered and that he must abandon the attempt on the capital. His personal briefing should stress the need to save face by capturing at least one of the three castles along the Toyokawa. For purposes of the game, Nagashino should become whichever castle Katsuyori besieges and seems likely to capture, whereupon Oda Nobunaga will decide to march to support Tokugawa Ieyasu, and a battle between the besiegers and the relief force will ensue.

The principal players will, obviously, take the roles of Takeda Katsuyori at Asuke, Tokugawa Ieyasu at Hamamatsu, Sadai Tadatsugu at Yoshida castle, Okudaira Sadamasa at Nagashino castle and Oda Nobunaga. Other players could portray their relatives and vassals, so that the game could depict not just stategic manoeuvres, but also the initial raising of armies, involving the calculating and negotiating of troop contingents by reference to land holdings, and questions of clan/vassal loyalty and the possibility of treachery.

The siege of Nagashino

Siege wargames usually require different structures to portray different aspects of the conflict: the lengthy processes of erecting siege lines,

RIGHT **It is quite amazing to consider that in spite of the huge number of casualties at Nagashino the Takeda still managed to pose a threat to Oda Nobunaga until 1582. Takeda Katsuyori was finally defeated at the battle of Temmokuzan. This fine print is a different depiction of Katsuyori's last moments. In this version his loyal retainers hold off the enemy as he prepares for death.**

二十一
天目山ノ
武田伊賀四郎勝家
主従 討死ス

bombardment, mining and starving out are best portrayed on maps or small-scale models in an umpire-controlled kriegsspiel, in which each turn represents one day; sorties by the garrison and attempts to carry outworks by storm can be recreated using 15mm or 25mm figures on a scale model of the appropriate part of the fortress. The contests for the various enclosures of Nagashino castle are eminently suitable for the latter type of game.

Existing commercial rules for medieval, fantasy or 16th-18th century European siege warfare can be easily adapted for this scenario, or a set of rules can be written specifically for the game.

Messages to Okazaki

The player commanding the Nagashino garrison will, at some stage, wish to send a messenger to Tokugawa Ieyasu. Escaping through the Takeda siege lines and returning if necessary can become a small, but entertaining game for a few players to enliven the slow progress of the siege, by employing the 'Forest Fight' system devised originally by Andy Callan for the French and Indian War.

The volunteer must elude pursuit by three groups of Takeda troops, each comprising one samurai and two or three ashigaru, not more than one of whom may be armed with an arquebus or bow. The playing surface or gameboard must be suitably painted and decorated with model trees to represent the forest around Nagashino castle. It comprises numbered identical sized squares, the faces of which are labelled A, B, C and D (or suitable Japanese characters that can be easily distinguished by the players), arranged in a random sequence – perhaps by the players taking turns to draw them from a bag or pile – that bears only a coincidental relationship to the true arrangement shown on a secret chart kept by the umpire.

At the start of the game, 15mm or 25mm figures portraying the messenger and his pursuers are placed on their respective starting positions. Each player in turn is invited by the umpire to nominate the face by which he proposes to leave the square currently occupied by his figure or figures. The umpire then consults his chart and places all the figures into those squares into which they have moved, which may well not be any of those adjacent to their starting positions. The messenger must endeavour to traverse the gameboard without being caught to exit by a particular square, whereupon he will be deemed to have eluded pursuit and be able to deliver his message to Tokugawa Ieyasu. The Takeda troops must try to stop him, by entering the same square as the messenger and defeating him in hand to hand combat. The umpire can, at his discretion, allow the ashigaru matchlockman or bowman to shoot at the messenger if the latter is moving across an adjacent square on the secret chart and the ashigaru is facing in the right direction to catch a glimpse of him. Combat can be resolved using simple skirmish rules, variants of 'Paper, Scissors, Stone' or other systems devised for the occasion. A return journey by the same messenger should be played with the squares in different positions, but the same umpire chart. In such a case the Takeda may nominate certain squares as containing traps before play commences. Attempts by different messengers require the creation of a new chart, however.

Such a game can be played to determine whether the Nagashino garrison summons assistance successfully, whether it learns that a relief force is on its way, and whether the Takeda besiegers also learn this fact, before one of the battle games described below. Suitably adapted and extended, this game might also be used to recreate the exploits of Torii Sune'emon.

Battle at Shidarahara

The obvious problem if one is trying to recreate a battle, whether it be Nagashino or Agincourt, in which one army launched an attack, which hindsight suggests was probably doomed to fail, is how to persuade one player, or a player team, to make such a charge when the outcome can be predicted?

One could endeavour to recruit players who are interested in samurai warfare of an earlier period, but have little or no knowledge of the Sengoku-jidai and this particular campaign.

The briefing for Takeda Katsuyori must encourage him to believe in the efficacy of his cavalry, emphasise the defeat of the Tokugawa at Mikata-ga-hara in 1572 and downplay the tactical importance of firearms in battles, but stress the necessity of using his own arquebus corps to maintain the siege of Nagashino castle. His aim must be to drive the relief forces of Tokugawa Ieyasu and Oda Nobunaga off quickly, before they can establish themselves in the area.

Oyamada Nobushige, who led 200 horsemen on the left wing of the charge at Nagashino, managed to survive the battle and escaped to his castle at Iwadono. In 1582, when the Tokugawa pressed home their attack into the Takeda territories, Takeda Katsuyori fled to Iwadono, only to find the gates closed against him.

ABOVE **The death of Oda Nobunaga. Having had the satisfaction of contemplating the head of Takeda Katsuyori, Oda Nobunaga did not have long to enjoy his triumph, because in that same year he was murdered in the Honnôji temple in Kyôto by Akechi Mitsuhide, one of his generals. In this dramatic print by Yoshitoshi Oda Nobunaga uses his bow and arrows as the temple blazes around him. (Courtesy of Rolf Degener).**

Oda Nobunaga's briefing must describe in detail the tactical lessons he has learned from campaigning against the Ikkô-ikki – the efficacy of arquebus volley fire by ashigaru or peasant troops when secure inside field fortifications – and his troops' use of long nagae-yari as units of pikemen. It should explain how a palisade can break up a cavalry charge into small groups of samurai horsemen, who can then be despatched by his own samurai and ashigaru.

Another possibility would be to disguise the scenario for the Takeda players, whilst remaining within the Sengoku-jidai, so that they believe they are playing an earlier battle – such as Mikata-ga-hara, perhaps – and so have either no knowledge of, or a poor opinion of, firearms and cannot anticipate their use en masse by Nobunaga's troops.

Alternatively, the Game Organiser can avoid the whole issue, without attempting to disguise the battle being fought, by adopting a game structure in which only one side is actively played.

The Takeda army could be programmed by the umpire to act historically, and all players would command contingents in the Oda-Tokugawa forces. The initial charges by the Takeda cavalry would become a 'space invaders' type shooting contest, followed by a mêlée, which would then focus on the personal experience of individual samurai and their retainers in hand to hand combat, as described below.

Another idea would be to recreate the perspective of individual Takeda samurai and their retainers in the charge, as a combined skirmish/roleplay game. The effect of volley fire from Oda Nobunaga's matchlock armed ashigaru would be determined by die rolls in conjunction with wound tables created specially for the game, based upon the results of the experiments described in this book. [See my appendices to *Balaclava 1854* and *Alexander 334-323BC* in the Campaign

This life sized reproduction of the charge of the Takeda cavalry at Nagashino is at the Ise Sengoku Jidai Mura. The dummies are made of fibre glass. During the daily performance the horsemen are bombarded with fire and smoke from fibre glass ashigaru.

LEFT The reconstructed fence at Nagashino viewed from about 200 metres away across the Rengogawa. This is about the maximum range for the arquebuses to do real damage, but firing probably did not begin until the horsemen had crossed the river.

Series for further ideas for gaming an individual cavalryman's experience of battle]

In either case, to ensure an enjoyable game, but unbeknown to the players, during the early charges the umpire would only implement mortal or disabling wounds upon horses, non-played characters and retainers, so as to keep players, who might be lightly wounded, in the game for as long as possible – at least until the Takeda cavalry reached or penetrated the palisade and engaged in hand to hand fighting with umpire-controlled Oda-Tokugawa samurai and ashigaru. Players could dice to summon the assistance of their personal retainers (provided they had not been killed or wounded already) in the mêlée. Each player's personal objective would be to survive, or die an honourable death and take as many heads heads of the enemy as possible.

Should the Game Organiser and the players, however, prefer a wargame in which both sides are controlled by the participants, it will probably be necessary to structure the recreation to commence only after the volley fire has decimated the Takeda cavalry, so that the game portrays the subsequent mêlée. This stage of the battle could be gamed in two ways, depending upon the players' tastes and the resources available.

A display of the entire Shidarahara battlefield, using small-scale – 1/300 or 6mm – models or troop counters for each contingent could be used to create the generals' perspective. Figures representing the tsukai-ban would be used to deliver the commanders' orders to troops not under their personal control. Combat would be controlled using stylised rules such as DBR.

A wooden lookout tower such as would have been used at Nagashino castle. This reconstruction is at Ise Sengoku Jidai Mura

Alternatively, the game could focus on the experience of just one clan within the battle in a tactical game with 15mm or 25mm models: the obvious choice, to offer a fairly even chance of success to both sides, would be to recreate the attack by Yamagata Masakage upon Oda Nobunaga's right wing, unprotected by the palisade, commanded by Okubo Tadayo.

Attack on the forts of Tobigasuyama

Sakai Tadatsugu's attack upon Takeda Nobuzane's forts of Nakayama and Tobigasu should be refought simultaneously with the action at Shidarahara, but out of sight and earshot of the players of the latter, as either a figure game or a kriegsspiel. The result should only be communicated to the Takeda players at the end of the main battle. Once Tadatsugu's troops have captured or set fire to Tobigasu, the sortie by Okudaira Sadamasa's garrison may also be fought out, if desired. These actions could also be fought as a self-contained game, in which the battle at Shidarahara is not played, but assumed to be following its historical course.

Finally, a complete disguise!

To conclude, here is a radically different approach for readers who neither possess nor wish to acquire samurai armies: set the campaign in the Wars of the Roses! This will avoid the problem of trying to create a non-European atmosphere for this wargame. For the daimyô who fought at Nagashino, just as for the 15th century English nobility, the campaign was part of a long power struggle between leading families for territory and effective control of the government.

So, let the Shogun be Henry VI, Takeda Katsuyori the Earl of Warwick, 'The Kingmaker', and Tokugawa Ieyasu and Oda Nobunaga two noblemen who support the House Of York. Nagashino becomes a medieval castle, the samurai, knights and men at arms and the ashigaru English yeomen archers, spearmen and handgunners. Scale down the forces to a size more suited to the Wars of the Roses and let battle commence – in this setting the tactical ploy of palisade and volley fire, whilst technologically possible, will not be suspected.

COMPANION SERIES FROM OSPREY

MEN-AT-ARMS
An unrivalled source of information on the organisation, uniforms and equipment of the world's fighting men, past and present. The series covers hundreds of subjects spanning 5,000 years of history. Each 48-page book includes concise texts packed with specific information, some 40 photos, maps and diagrams, and eight colour plates of uniformed figures.

ELITE
Detailed information on the uniforms and insignia of the world's most famous military forces. Each 64-page book contains some 50 photographs and diagrams, and 12 pages of full-colour artwork.

NEW VANGUARD
Comprehensive histories of the design, development and operational use of the world's armoured vehicles and artillery. Each 48-page book contains eight pages of full-colour artwork including a detailed cutaway.

WARRIOR
Definitive analysis of the armour, weapons, tactics and motivation of the fighting men of history. Each 64-page book contains cutaways and exploded artwork of the warrior's weapons and armour.

ORDER OF BATTLE
The most detailed information ever published on the units which fought history's great battles. Each 96-page book contains comprehensive organisation diagrams supported by ultra-detailed colour maps. Each title also includes a large fold-out base map.

AIRCRAFT OF THE ACES
Focuses exclusively on the elite pilots of major air campaigns, and includes unique interviews with surviving aces sourced specifically for each volume. Each 96-page volume contains up to 40 specially commissioned artworks, unit listings, new scale plans and the best archival photography available.

COMBAT AIRCRAFT
Technical information from the world's leading aviation writers on the aircraft types flown. Each 96-page volume contains up to 40 specially commissioned artworks, unit listings, new scale plans and the best archival photography available.